Killing Kennedy
The Real Story

Dedicated to Brave & Dune

Also by the author

Hip Hop
Art After Midnight
Cannabis Cures Cancer?
The Bitcoin Revolution
The Ultimate Film Guide
Killing Lincoln: The Real Story
Magic, Religion & Cannabis
Hip Hop: The Complete Archives
1966
Treasure of the Holy Grail

Introduction to an Assassination

Kennedy had little clue to the trap he was riding into.

Although John F. Kennedy was neither a saint nor a great intellectual, he was the youngest President ever elected, which may explain why he was so well attuned to the changing mood of America in the Sixties. Americans had grown weary of Cold War hysteria. They wanted to relax and have fun. Like the majority of people across the planet, they wanted peace.

The President's primary obstacle in this quest was a massive, power-hungry bureaucracy that had emerged after WWII—a Frankenstein monster created by anti-Communist paranoia and inflated defense budgets. By 1960, the Pentagon was easily the world's largest corporation, with assets of over $60 billion. No one understood this monster better than President Dwight D. Eisenhower. On January 17, 1961, in his farewell address to the nation, Eisenhower spoke to the country, and to his successor, John Kennedy.

"The conjunction of an immense military establishment and a large arms industry is new in the American experience," said Eisenhower. "We must guard against the acquisition of unwarranted influence, whether sought or unsought, by the military-industrial complex."

At the beginning of his administration, Kennedy seems to have followed the advice of his military and intelligence officers. What else could such a young and inexperienced President have done? Signs of a serious rift, however, first appeared after the Bay of Pigs, a CIA-planned-and-executed invasion of Cuba that took place three months after Kennedy took office. The invasion was so bungled Kennedy refused to send American forces to save the day and immediately afterward fired CIA Director Allen Dulles, Deputy Director General Charles Cabell and Deputy Director of Planning Richard Bissell. Since Dulles was David Rockefeller's cousin (by marriage), and had long been a major force in the national security system along with his brother John Foster, firing Dulles was probably not a wise move and certainly contributed to the events that followed.

Edward Lansdale, former OSS and Air Force officer, was brought back from Vietnam to assist with anti-Cuban operations. Lansdale had previously supervised the secret recovery of vast amounts of treasure stolen by the Japanese which had been stashed in the Philippines during the war's end. Locating the booby-trapped treasure sites and removing the contents had been the best-kept postwar secret as billions were carefully placed in secret accounts around the globe, a highly illegal operation devised by Secretary of War Henry Stimson.

After securing this treasure, Lansdale quickly became an expert in psychological warfare by supervising public relations campaigns (terror ops) in various Asian countries. One of the CIA's most gung-ho boom-and-bang cowboys, Bill Harvey, was placed in charge of Task Force W (the heart of the anti-Cuban campaign), and Harvey picked his associate Theodore Shackley to run JM/Wave, which quickly became the CIA's largest and best-funded station. A former Navy blimp port located south of Miami on 1,500 wooded acres, it became known as Zenith Technological Enterprises. By the spring of 1962, ZTE had over 200 officers and 2,200 Cuban mercenaries on its payroll, a navy of over 100 craft, and access to F-105 Phantoms from nearby Homestead Air Force Base. Harvey contracted a well-known mobster originally from Chicago named Johnny Roselli to help them assassinate Castro. The CIA and the Sicilian men-of-honor had a common enemy in Castro and the necessary introductions had been provided by the former second-in-command of the FBI's Chicago office, Robert Maheu.

In September, the Joint Chiefs submitted their already-approved operation titled Northwoods for JFK's review, an operation involving numerous acts of false-flag terrorism to be blamed on Cuba as a pretense for an invasion. JFK was horrified and fired the head of the Joint Chiefs in retaliation. Alarmed by the removal of the heads of the CIA and Pentagon, powerful forces began to coalesce, inspired and assisted by a far-right, anti-Communist organization, the John Birch Society.

Kennedy's next major crisis occurred on October 16, 1962, when he was shown aerial photographs of missile bases under construction in Cuba. The Joint Chiefs and CIA pressed for an immediate attack. Instead, Attorney General Robert Kennedy was sent to meet with Soviet Ambassador Anatoly Dobrynin. In his memoirs, Soviet Premier Nikita Krushchev quoted the younger Kennedy as saying, "The President is in a grave situation. We are under pressure from our military to use force against Cuba.... If the situation continues much longer, the President is not sure that the military will not overthrow him and seize power."

U2 spy plane photograph of Cuban missile base.

Military hopes for an invasion of Cuba evaporated as Krushchev and Kennedy worked out a nonviolent solution to the crisis. In return, Kennedy promised not to invade Cuba and also secretly removed nuclear missiles from US bases in Turkey, which had to enrage the Pentagon.

Angered over the Bay of Pigs fiasco, the CIA's mercenary army refused to bend to Kennedy's will and sought to continue the destabilization campaign against Castro, which included sabotage raids. A bitter internal struggle developed around Kennedy's attempts to disband the paramilitary operations in Florida and Louisiana. Task Group W, the CIA's massive anti-Cuban operation suddenly lost all funding and Lansdale was told to clear out his desk at the Pentagon.

On August 5, 1963, the US, Great Britain and the Soviet Union signed a limited nuclear test ban treaty. Engineered by President Kennedy and long in negotiation, the treaty was a severe blow to the cold warriors in the Pentagon and CIA. On September 20, 1963, Kennedy spoke hopefully of peace to the UN General Assembly. "Today we may have reached a pause in the Cold War," he said. "If both sides can now gain new confidence and experience in concrete collaborations of peace, then surely, this first small step can be the start of a long, fruitful journey."

"Years later, paging through its formerly classified records, talking to the National Security Council staff, it is difficult to avoid the impression that the President was learning the responsibilities of power," writes John Pradow in *Keeper of the Keys*, an analysis of the National Security Council. "Here is a smoother, calmer Kennedy, secretly working for rapprochement with Fidel Castro and a withdrawal from Vietnam."

Although Kennedy's Vietnam policy did not receive widespread publicity, he turned resolutely against the war in June of 1963, when he ordered Defense Secretary Robert McNamara and Chairman of the Joint Chiefs Maxwell Taylor to announce from the White House steps that all American forces would be withdrawn by 1965. At the time, 15,500 "advisors" were stationed in South Vietnam, and total casualties suffered remained a relatively low 100.

On November 14, Kennedy signed an order to begin the withdrawal by removing 1,000 troops. In private, Kennedy let it be known that the military was not going to railroad him into continuing the war. Many of the hardline, anti-Communists—including FBI Director J. Edgar Hoover—would have to be purged. Bobby Kennedy would be in charge of dismantling the CIA, an agency that could not be trusted to carry out the President's agenda. President Kennedy told Senator Mike Mansfield of his plans to tear the CIA "into a thousand pieces and scatter it to the wind." But these plans had to wait for Kennedy's reelection in 1964. And in order to win that election, he had to secure the South, which is why Kennedy went to Texas later that month.

Marine takes custody of suspected Viet Cong.

Could Kennedy have stopped the war in Vietnam, as we his obvious intention? America will never know. His command to begin the Vietnam withdrawal was his last formal executive order. Just after noon on November 22, President Kennedy was murdered while driving through downtown Dallas, in full view of dozens of ardent supporters, and while surrounded by police and personal bodyguards. Decades later, grave doubts still linger about who pulled the triggers, who ordered the assassination, who paid for it, and why our government has done so little to bring justice forth.

In 1963, no American wanted to believe that President Kennedy's death was a *coup d'etat*, planned by the military establishment and executed by a renegade CIA station working with a Sicilian secret society. Today, such a claim can no longer be dismissed as evidence over the years continues to support this thesis. Twenty years ago, tremendous strides in uncovering the truth were made by Oliver Stone's film *JFK*. As his focal point for the story, Stone chose former New Orleans District Attorney Jim Garrison, the only prosecutor to attempt to bring this case to court, and a man subjected to one of the most effective smear campaigns ever orchestrated by the US government. It is a frightening story of murder, corruption and cover-up. Even today, decades after he brought the case to court, a powerful media disinformation campaign against Garrison continues.

Earling "Jim" Carothers Garrison.

Born November 20, 1921, in Knoxville, Iowa, Earling Garrison—known as "Jim" to his friends and family—was raised in New Orleans. At age 19, one year after Pearl Harbor, he joined the army. In 1942, he was sent to Europe, where he volunteered to fly spotter planes over the front lines. Following the war, he attended law school at Tulane, joined the FBI and served as a special agent in Seattle and Tacoma. After growing bored with his agency assignments, he returned to New Orleans to practice law and served as an assistant district attorney from 1954 to 1958.

In 1961, Garrison decided to run for district attorney on a platform openly hostile to then New Orleans Mayor Victor Schiro. To the surprise of many, he was elected without any major political backing. At 43, he had been district attorney for less than two years when Kennedy was killed. "I was an old-fashioned patriot," he writes in *On the Trail of the Assassins*, "a product of my family, my military experience, and my years in the legal profession. I could not imagine then that the government would ever deceive the citizens of this country."

A few hours after the assassination, Lee Harvey Oswald was arrested. Two days later, while in Dallas police custody, Oswald was murdered by nightclub owner Jack Ruby. Garrison learned that Oswald was from New Orleans, and arranged a Sunday afternoon meeting with his staff. With such an important case, it was their responsibility to investigate Oswald's local connections.

David Ferrie.

Within days, they learned Oswald had recently been seen in the company of David Ferrie, a fervent anti-Communist and freelance pilot linked to the Bay of Pigs invasion. Evidence placed Ferrie in

13

Texas on the day of the assassination. Also on that day, a friend of Ferrie's named Guy Bannister (former head of the Chicago FBI) had pistol-whipped one Jack Martin during an argument. Martin confided to friends that Bannister and Ferrie were somehow involved in the assassination. Garrison had Ferrie picked up for questioning, and turned him over to the local FBI, who immediately released him. Within a few months, the Warren Commission released its report stating that Oswald was a lone nut murdered by a misguided patriot who wanted to spare Jackie Kennedy the ordeal of testifying. Like most Americans at the time, Garrison accepted this farfetched conclusion.

Three years later, in the fall of 1966, Garrison was happily married with three children, and content with his job, when a chance conversation with Senator Russell Long changed his views on the Warren Commission forever.

"Those fellows on the Warren Commission were dead wrong," said Long. "There's no way in the world that one man could have shot up Jack Kennedy that way."

Intrigued, Garrison went back to his office and ordered the complete 26-volume report. "The mass of information was disorganized and confused," writes Garrison. "Worst of all, the conclusions in the report seemed to be based on an appallingly selective reading of the evidence, ignoring credible testimony from literally dozens of witnesses."

Garrison equally disturbed by the background of the men chosen by President Johnson to serve on the commission. Why, for instance, was Dulles, a man recently fired by Kennedy, on the panel? A master spy during WWII, Dulles had orchestrated the surveillance of the Abwehr (Hitler's military intelligence agency). In the final days of the war, he'd supervised the secret surrender of the elite Nazi SS Corps, and he'd also played a major role in the subsequent incorporation of hundreds of Nazi war criminals, scientists and spies into the newly formed CIA. He was powerful, well-connected to Wall Street and had been director of the CIA for eight years. Certainly, he was no friend to John Kennedy. Serving with Dulles were Representative Gerald Ford, a man described by *Newsweek* as "the CIA's best friend in Congress," John McCloy, former assistant secretary of war, and Senator Richard Russell, chairman of the powerful Senate Armed Services Committee. Russell's home state of Georgia was peppered with military bases and military-industrial contracts. The balance of the commission was clearly in the hands of the military and the CIA. The investigation was supervised by Hoover, who openly detested the Kennedy brothers. It looked like a typical snow-job with any useful evidence buried under an avalanche of meaningless detail (the same technique, in fact, the Union War Department had deployed a century earlier to bury the backstory on the Lincoln assassination).

Another interesting link turned up. The mayor of Dallas was Earle Cabell, brother of General Charles Cabell, whom JFK had earlier fired from the CIA. Earle Cabell was in a position to control many important details involved in the case, including the Dallas police force.

Based on these general suspicions, Garrison launched a highly secret investigation around Oswald's links to Ferrie and Bannister. Unfortunately, Bannister had died nine months after the assassination. An alcoholic and rabid right-winger, Bannister had been a former naval intelligence operative and a star agent for the FBI. He was a leader in the spook-infested John Birch Society and the Minutemen, another right-wing organization, and publisher of a racist newsletter. His office at 544 Camp Street was a well-known meeting place for anti-Castro Cubans.

Ferrie's background was even more bizarre. A former senior pilot for Eastern Airlines, Ferrie had been head of the New Orleans Civil Air Patrol, an organization Oswald had joined as a teenager. Many of the boys in the Civil Air Patrol willingly had themselves hypnotized by Ferrie, supposedly to improve their skills and ability to withstand pain. Some attended homosexual orgies at Ferrie's house. When complaints concerning these events were filed with the New Orleans police, however, Ferrie somehow had the investigations quashed, despite rampant evidence there was child abuse involved. Another teenager involved with the group was Barry Seal, and many decades later, he would be unveiled as the country's biggest drug smuggler.

Guy Bannister.

Ferrie suffered from alopecia, an ailment that left him hairless. He wore bright red wigs and painted his eyebrows. He founded his own religion, and kept hundreds of rats in cages for experiments on weaponizing cancer. He'd flown dozens of solo missions for the CIA in Cuba and Latin America, and had links to Carlos Marcello, head of the Sicilian men-of-honor in Louisiana. Like Bannister, he was extremely rightwing. "I want to train killers," Ferrie had written to the commander of the US Air Force. "There's nothing I would enjoy better than blowing the hell out of every damn Russian, Communist, Red or what-have-you."

On the day of the assassination, Dean Andrews, a New Orleans attorney, had been asked to fly to Dallas to represent Oswald. When asked by the Warren Commission who'd hired him, Andrews replied "Clay Bertrand." Bertrand, Garrison discovered, was a pseudonym used by Clay Shaw, director of the International Trade Mart. Shaw, a darling of New Orleans high society, was also well-connected in high-finance circles. He was also an associate of Ferrie and Bannister. Like many others connected with this case, Shaw was a former Army intelligence officer. The case against Shaw was circumstantial, but Garrison did have an eyewitness willing to testify that Shaw had met with Lee Harvey Oswald just prior to the assassination.

Just as Garrison was marshaling his case, some strange events took place. On February 17, 1967, the New Orleans States-Item published a story on Garrison's secret probe, indicating he'd already spent over $8,000 of taxpayer's money investigation the Kennedy assassination. Soon thereafter, Garrison received an unusually strong letter of support from a Denver oil businessman named John Miller, hinting that Miller wanted to offer financial assistance to the investigation. When Miller arrived in New Orleans, he met with Garrison and one of his associates. "You're too big for this job," said Miller. "I suggest you accept an appointment to the bench in a federal district court, and move into a job more worthy of your talents."

"And what would I have to do to get this judgeship?" asked Garrison.

"Stop your investigation," replied Miller calmly.

Garrison asked Miller to leave his office.

"Well, they offered you the carrot and you turned it down," said his assistant. "You know what's coming next don't you?"

Suddenly, reporters from all over the country descended on New Orleans, including Washington Post contributor George Lardner, Jr. At midnight on February 22, 1967, Lardner said he conducted a four-hour interview with Ferrie. The following morning, Ferrie was found dead. Two unsigned, typewritten suicide notes were found. One letter made reference to a "messianic district attorney."

Three days later the coroner announced Ferrie had died of natural causes and placed the time of death well before the end of Lardner's marathon interview. Lardner's possible complicity in the affair would never be called into question, while his highly influential article in the *Washington Post* branded Garrison's investigation a fraud. It was just the beginning of a long series of disruptive attacks in the media, and the first of many people connected to the case that would mysteriously turn up dead.

With Ferrie gone, Garrison had only one suspect left. He rushed his case to court, arresting Clay Shaw.

Clay Shaw.

Ellen Ray, a documentary filmmaker from New York, came to New Orleans to film the story. "People were getting killed left and right," she recalls. "Garrison would subpoena a witness and two days later the witness would be killed by a parked car. I thought

Garrison was a great American patriot. But things got a little too heavy when I started getting strange phone calls from men with Cuban accents." After several death threats, Ray became so terrified that instead of making the documentary on the trial, she fled the country.

David Ferrie (2nd from left) and Lee Harvey Oswald (far right)

Attorney General Ramsey Clark, a close friend of President Lyndon Johnson, announced from Washington that the federal government had already investigated and exonerated Clay Shaw. "Needless to say," writes Garrison, "this did not exactly make me look like District Attorney of the Year."

Meanwhile, the Justice Department began backpedaling. If Shaw had been investigated, why wasn't his name in the Warren Commission Report? "The Attorney General has since determined that this was erroneous," said a spokesman for Clark. "Nothing arose indicating a need to investigate Mr. Shaw."

Realizing he was in a political minefield, Garrison presented his case as cautiously as possible. A grand jury was convened that included Jay C. Albarado. "On March 14, three criminal-court judges heard Garrison's case in a preliminary hearing to determine if there was enough evidence against Shaw to hold him for trial," Albarado wrote many years later in a letter to the New Orleans *Times-Picayune*. "What did they conclude? That there was sufficient evidence. Garrison then presented his evidence to a 12-member grand jury. We ruled there was sufficient evidence to bring Shaw to trial. Were we duped by Garrison? I think not."

Thanks to all the unwanted publicity, Garrison's staff had swollen with volunteers eager to work on the case. The 6'6" Garrison, now dubbed the "Jolly Green Giant," had already become a hero to many citizens and researchers who had serious doubts about the Warren Commission. Unfortunately, a few of these eager volunteers were later exposed as government informers. Shortly before the case went to trial, one of the infiltrators copied all of Garrison's files and turned them over to Shaw's defense team.

On September 4, 1967, Supreme Court Justice Earl Warren announced that Garrison's case was worthless. The *New York Times* characterized the investigation as a "morbid frolic." *Newsweek* reported that the conspiracy was "a plot of Garrison's own making." *Life* magazine published the first of many reports linking Garrison with the mafia. (Richard Billings, an editor at *Life*, had been one of the first journalists to gain access to Garrison's inner circle, under the guise of "wanting to help" the investigation.) Walter Sheridan, a former naval intelligence operative and NBC investigator, appeared in New Orleans with a film crew. Their purpose? An expose titled The Case of Jim Garrison, which was broadcast in June 1967. "It required only a few minutes to see that NBC had classified the case as criminal and had appointed itself as the prosecutor," wrote Garrison.

Puzzled by the intensity of NBC's attack, Garrison went to the library and did some research on the company. He learned the network was a subsidiary of RCA, a bulwark of the military-industrial complex whose defense contracts had increased by more than a billion dollars from 1960 to 1967. Its chairman, retired General David Sarnoff, was a well-known proponent of the Cold War.

"Some long-cherished illusions about the great free press in our country underwent a painful reappraisal during this period," wrote Garrison.

Clay Shaw was brought to trial on January 29, 1969. It took less than one month for Garrison to present his case.

Demonstrating the cover-up was the easy part. Although the overwhelming majority of eyewitnesses at Dealey Plaza testified that the fatal shot came not from the Texas School Book Depository—where Oswald worked—but from a grassy knoll overlooking the plaza, the FBI had encouraged many witnesses to alter their testimony to fit the "lone nut" theory. Those that didn't were simply ignored by the Commission. The ballistic evidence was flawed and obviously tampered with. Even though the FBI had received several warnings of the assassination, they had been ignored. Security for the President was strangely lax. Although Oswald's killer, Jack Ruby, had ties to the CIA and the Chicago Sicilian men-of-honor society, this evidence had been suppressed. Ruby was never allowed to testify before the Commission. When interviewed in a Texas jail by Chief Justice Warren and Gerald Ford, he told them, "I would like to request that I go to Washington.... I want to tell the truth, and I can't tell it here.... Gentlemen, my life is in danger." Ruby never made it to Washington. He remained in jail and died mysteriously before Garrison could depose him as a witness.

Even more disturbing was the treatment given the deceased President's corpse. Under Texas law, an autopsy should have been performed by a civilian pathologist in Dallas. Instead, the body was removed at gunpoint by the Secret Service and flown to a Navy hospital in Maryland, where an incomplete autopsy was performed under supervision of unnamed admirals and generals, the notes of which were quickly burned. Bullet holes were never tracked, the brain was not dissected, and organs were not removed. The autopsy was a botched, tainted affair, performed under military supervision. (The medical aspects of the case were so weird, they would later form the basis for a best-selling book, *Best Evidence* by David Lifton.)

The most important and lasting piece of evidence unveiled by Garrison was an 8mm film of the assassination taken by Abraham Zapruder, a film that only three members of the Warren Commission had seen, probably because it cast a long shadow of doubt across their conclusions. A good analysis was written by J. Gary Shaw and Larry Harris, in *Cover-Up*:

"Had the Zapruder film of the JFK assassination been shown on national television Friday evening, November 22, 1963, the Oswald/lone assassin fabrication would have been unacceptable to a majority of Americans.... The car proceeds down Elm and briefly disappears behind a sign. When it emerges the President has obviously been shot.... Governor Connally turns completely to the right, looking into the back seat; he begins to turn back when his body stiffens on impact of a bullet. Very shortly after Connally is hit, the President's head explodes in a shower of blood and brain matter—he is driven violently backward at a speed estimated at 80-100 feet per second."

Although Time, Inc. could have made a small fortune distributing this film around the world, they instead secured the rights from Zapruder for $225,000, then held a few private screenings before locking it in a vault. It was shown to one newsman, Dan Rather, who then described it on national television. Rather asserted that Kennedy's went "forward with considerable force" after the fatal head shot (a statement that would have supported a hit from behind, from the direction of the School Book Depository. Several months later, Rather was promoted to White House Correspondent by CBS. As if to buttress this fabrication, the FBI reversed the order of the frames when printing them in the Warren Report. When researchers later drew this reversal to the FBI's attention, Hoover attributed the switch to a "printing error."

Although Garrison proved his conspiracy, the jury was not convinced of Clay Shaw's role in it. He was released after only two hours of deliberation.

The end of the Clay Shaw trial was just the beginning of a long nightmare for Garrison. On June 30, 1971, he was arrested by federal agents on corruption charges. Two years later, the case came to trial at the height of Garrison's reelection campaign. Although he won the case, he lost the election by 2,000 votes. However, the Jolly Green Giant remained widely respected in his home state, and was later elected to two terms on the second-highest court in Louisiana.

In 1967, the machinations of the CIA were unknown to most Americans. Today, thankfully, a few brave men have left their comfortable careers in the agency and spoken out against CIA-sponsored terror around the world. Unfortunately, many of these are undoubtedly just playing a role. When whistleblowers end up on the cover of *Time* magazine, it's safe to assume they are an intel dangle seeding limited hang-outs, and not real whistleblowers. *Time* magazine was created by a member of Yale University's notorious Skull & Bones society, viewed as a steppingstone into the star chamber.

Victor Marchetti was a former executive assistant to CIA director Richard Helms and subsequently coauthored *The CIA and the Cult of Intelligence* with John D. Marks. Marchetti confirmed

Shaw and Ferrie had been CIA assets, and that the agency had worked secretly for Shaw's defense during the Garrison investigation. When Marchetti left the CIA, he began writing for *The Spotlight*, run by the Liberty Lobby, where he joined another former intelligence officer, Mark Lane, who had appeared in Dallas to offer pro bono assistance to Oswald's widow. Founded in 1958 by Willis Carto, the Liberty Lobby funded the birth of the holocaust denial movement and bore familiar signatures of a counterintelligence propaganda operation. But then 90% of material written about the assassination appears to either have been created to cast mud on the case, defend the Warren Commission, or brand researchers as crackpots.

Mark Lane in Ann Arbor in 1967.

A few inside the military have tried to speak out, but the real ones probably ended up dead. Retired Colonel L. Fletcher Prouty, Chief of Special Operations for the Joint Chiefs until 1964, became one of the most well-known critics of the Warren Commission. Prouty claimed he was on assignment in New Zealand on the day of the assassination, and after carrying a New Zealand newspaper article back to Washington, checked the time of Oswald's arrest against the hour the paper had been printed and realized Oswald's biography had gone out over the international newswire before Oswald was arrested by the Dallas police. Until his death in June 2001, Prouty remained a persistent critic of the Warren Commission, but never really penetrated the truth in significant detail. His book *The Secret Team* is difficult to follow, as was Mark Lane's *Rush to Judgment*. Even though these two correctly identified the CIA as the major culprit early on, they never shined any light on Harvey or Shackley, and instead diverted attention toward Hunt.

On March 6, 1975, the Zapruder film made its national television debut on ABC's *Good Night America*. As a result of this long-delayed national screening, enough public pressure was put on Congress to reopen the case. Unfortunately, this investigation became as carefully manipulated as the Warren Commission, eventually falling under control of G. Robert Blakey, a man with close ties to the CIA. As could be expected, Blakey led the investigation away from the CIA and towards the Sicilian men-of-honor. Blakey's conclusion was the President Kennedy was killed as the result of a conspiracy, and that organized crime had the means, method and motive. "The Garrison investigation was a fraud," said Blakey. Richard Billings, the former *Time-Life* editor, was a prominent member of Blakey's staff.

However, a number of highly detailed books on the assassination later appeared, and the most credible support Garrison not Blakey. "Could the mafia have whisked Kennedy's body past the Texas authorities and got it aboard Air Force One?" wrote Garrison. "Could the mafia have placed in charge of the President's autopsy an army general who was not a physician? Could the mafia have arranged for President Kennedy's brain to disappear from the National Archives?"

Today, we know the CIA recruited assassins from within the Sicilian society. And we know some of these people were the actual shooters of JFK, while Cubans from the Bay of Pigs provided support staff. Shortly before his disappearance, Teamster

25

boss Jimmy Hoffa said, "Jim Garrison's a smart man. Anyone who thinks he's a kook is a look himself." Was Hoffa silenced because he knew too much about the plot? Just before their scheduled appearances before the House investigation in the mid-Seventies, Roselli and Giancana were murdered. While testifying in front of Congress, CIA-head Richard Helms admitted the retired Harvey was assumed to have been Giancana's executioner due to the close proximity of their residences. Once his boss was dead, Roselli lost his protection and fled to Florida, where his dismembered body was found floating in a barrel in Biscayne Bay.

In July 1988, *The Nation* published an FBI memorandum from Hoover dated November 29, 1963. Obtained through the Freedom of Information Act, the memo implicated "George Bush of the CIA" in the Kennedy assassination cover-up. Although former President George Bush Sr., denied any contact with the agency prior to his being named director in 1976, it is known today that Zapata, the oil company Bush founded in 1960, was a CIA front that built platforms in the Gulf of Mexico used as bases to launch attacks on Cuba.

Former President Richard Nixon is also implicated in the cover-up. Nixon was in Dallas the day before the assassination, and one of his fears during the early days of Watergate was the "Bay of Pigs thing" would be uncovered. At least, that is the card he tried to play with Helms to stop the investigation of Watergate. But today we know the CIA likely staged the Watergate scandal in order to remove Nixon from power. A possible motive may have been Nixon's détente move with China, which may have been bought with the bribe of returning a secret gold fund to China, gold stolen by the Japanese and hidden in the Philippines. Recovery of the stolen loot from WWII had been supervised by Secretary of War Henry Stimson, another member of Skull & Bones, who'd named it the Black Eagle Fund.

As liaison between the CIA and Pentagon during the Bay of Pigs, Fletcher Prouty had been put in charge of ordering supplies for the invasion. "The CIA had code named the invasion 'Zapata'" Prouty told me in 1988. "Two boats landed on the shores of Cuba. One named Houston, the other Barbara. They were Navy ships that had been repainted with new names. I have no idea where the new names came from." Unfortunately, this information later proved not entirely accurate, as I learned five freighters were used by Brigade 2506 at the Bay of Pigs: *Houston, Rio Escondido, Caribe, Atlantic* and *Lake Charles*. These troop transport vessels were supported by two better-armed boats, the *Blagar* and *Barbara J.*

Leon Fletcher Prouty.

If Garrison's investigation was not a fraud, it's reasonable to assume that high-placed individuals in the conspiracy would either be dead or would have obtained considerable power. According to an article in the March 4, 1991 issue of *U.S. News & World Report*, Nixon and Bush remained close associates. "Nixon is in contact with Bush or his senior staff every month," wrote Kenneth Walsh. "Nixon also speaks regularly on the phone with [National Security Adviser] Brent Scowcroft.... And Chief of Staff John Sununu."

In 1991, Len Colodny and Robert Gettlin published *Silent Coup*, an analysis of the real forces behind the Watergate scandal.

According to the authors, Nixon fell prey to a military coup after refusing to work with the Pentagon. Is this book real, or, like so much of what has been published on the case, just another example of a state-sponsored rabbit hole designed to muddy the investigative waters?

Carl Olgesby was probably one of the first researchers to study the tracks of the Nazi spies, scientists and war criminals who made their way into the CIA, secretly protected and shielded through an operation supervised by Dulles. Olgesby's hard-to-find book, *The Yankee-Cowboy War*, remains one of the best documents on the links between the JFK assassination and the Watergate scandal. Later on, John Loftus, a former U.S. Department of Justice Nazi War Crimes prosecutor, would unravel evidence the Rockefeller and Harriman fortunes had invested heavily in building up the Nazi war machine and maintained contracts with German corporations during and after the war. The principle bank through which this money flowed was New York's Union Bank. The bank's director, Prescott Bush, hired Dulles in 1937 as the attorney whose job it was to "cloak" the accounts.

In the Eighties, a researcher named Danny Casolaro would follow this research into a network he dubbed "The Octopus," a secret global organization he felt controlled much of the world's illegal drug traffic, arms trading and money laundering. In August 1991, Casolaro lost his life in his quest to uncover the heads of this Octopus. Today most researchers would add child prostitution, child pornography, child slavery, and the manufacture of Manchurian candidates through mind control to the list of crimes committed by this group.

One thing is for sure: a well-orchestrated disinformation campaign continues to dump mud into the investigative waters while sheep-dipping any real research as worthless "conspiracy theory." All the major media companies refuse to face reality. The American people are bombarded with information about the Kennedy assassination, almost all of which claims Oswald was not connected to the CIA asset and really did shoot the President. It's important to understand the avalanche of disinformation is proof of the cover-up. How extensive is the CIA's infiltration of the national media? In 1977, Carl Bernstein wrote an article in *Rolling Stone* that named over 400 journalists uncovered by the 1973 Senate Church Committee who worked for the CIA. If anything, these numbers have increased exponentially over the past decades as the iron grip of our national security state over the nation has intensified.

Danny Casolaro.

Will the subversion of the national media ever end? The hope is in the Internet, and whether the monopolies held by the major media companies will dissolve as people gradually find their way to the truth. I still hold hope alive that one day America will once again be the sweet land of liberty her founders intended us to be.

Proofs of a Conspiracy

Pristine bullet found on a stretcher in Parkland Hospital, which, according to the Warren Commission, magically passed through Kennedy's back, exited through his neck, and then broke a rib and shattered the wrist of Governor Connally before falling onto the stretcher. The slight gouge in the nose and base were created while extracting samples for testing.

Dulles & the Protocols

There's nothing quite like being born into an old money family, like Allen Dulles was. His grandfather was Secretary of State under President Harrison, while his uncle served that post for President Wilson. Dulles was cousin to David Rockefeller (by marriage), educated at Princeton and always a bit sensitive about his club foot.

I think Dulles became a spook right out of college, as he went directly into the Diplomatic Corps, a haven for spooks since its inception. He became sheep-dipped as a knight in shining armor by returning from Europe to help write an expose on the *Protocols of the Elders of Zion* in the *New York Times*. Since their appearance, the *Protocols* have been used as a counterintelligence tool to soften up populations by scapegoating Jews prior to instigating a violent pogrom. But Dulles didn't reveal that truth, just that whoever wrote the *Protocols* cribbed material from a variety of sources which means they weren't really the notes from some satanic world council of Jewish leaders. The *Protocols* claimed a global conspiracy was underfoot to secretly manifest a new world war designed to milk profits while killing millions of innocents in the process.

When old money has big plans for one of their knights, they run an op to have that person sheep-dipped into an icon quick as possible, sort of like the way John Kerry was run around the jungle in Vietnam to look like he was a heroic, dashing soldier in combat mode, when really he was just faking it for the cameras the whole time and never in any sort of danger.

When Dulles returned to New York, he went to work for the British and his job was to foment World War II and get America into the war as quickly as possible. It seems Dulles had friends on Wall Street who were funding the rise of Hitler and Communism in the hope of producing an epic clash of cultures that could be milked for profit for years. The military-industrial complex was but a glean in their eye and speck in their heart, but within a few years they would become the dominant force in America.

Allen Dulles.

The plan may have been to have Germany and Japan conquer most of the world while stealing everything possible and wreaking as much terror and havoc on civilians as possible (survivors are shell-shocked and easily manipulated by propaganda and intel ops). After Germany and Japan were vanquished, conquered profit streams and cartels could be divided amongst the victors on Wall Street and inside the Bank of England, although the old money families of Germany and Japan would be left with their corporations and family fortunes mostly intact, and Europe's dominant cartel, I.G. Farben, was merely split into a few pieces. (And by the way, Farben had been designed and set-up through loans engineered by Dulles' brother John Foster and based off its biggest corporate investor, Standard Oil.)

Meanwhile, the stolen loot could be secretly transferred around the Bank of International Settlements in a shell-game designed to conceal who-got-when-where-why. It was a win-win for some old money families. Just so you know, the favorite banker of the Nazis invented the Bank of International Settlements, and put it into place shortly before the war started, and located it in Switzerland.

When the war broke out, Dulles was moved to Switzerland to conduct operations against Germany. The reason the German resistance failed internally was not because many Germans did not want to get rid of the maniac Hitler, a demagogue old money had put into power, but because Dulles and SIS refused to take the German resistance to Hitler seriously and let vital intelligence assets like Count Von Stauffenberg and Wilhelm Canaris dangle around helpless until the SS could round them up and assassinate them. Every single attempt to warn British and American intelligence about Hitler's plans was ignored. The fact Stauffenberg and Canaris were both assassinated leaves no doubt they were high-ranking aristocrats working hard to neutralize Hitler, but died without receiving a shred of support from his supposed enemies. Support that could have brought an early end to the war.

When the war was over, Dulles imported the cream of Nazi scientists, spooks and assassins and employed them to help build the Central Intelligence Agency, which was constructed with the assistance of his old boss from British intelligence and modeled after MI5-6, with the key component of a counterintelligence unit for dirty tricks. Dulles put his close friend James Angleton in this crucial post because Angleton had been posted in Italy while Dulles was in Switzerland and had been trained by British intelligence and maintained close relations with the Vatican, which was providing crucial support to help shelter Nazis until they could be moved to new positions in North and South

America. Before getting this job, Angleton promised never to put Dulles or any of his cronies on Wall Street on a lie detector and ask questions about their relations with German corporations during the war.

Just to give you an idea of what was going on, the Luftwaffe depended on Standard Oil for the war's entire duration and could not have flown without it. Since Standard was owned by Dulles' cousin (by marriage), one can see how easily these two people could have conspired to manifest and conceal illegal profits by playing both sides against the middle, which is standard black ops for British intelligence.

Another revealing detail is Farben was the dominant industrial, chemical and fuel corporation in Europe, and held a virtual monopoly in Europe on all things petrochemical, and yet its immense headquarters housing 200,000 workers was never bombed during the war. Now consider immediately after the war, the US Army Command moved into Farben's executive offices. Hitler had tried to blow up German's infrastructure in a fit of depression, but Hitler couldn't blow up I.G. Farben. That was run by old money and some of Farben's biggest investors were back in New York City.

Maybe you haven't figured this out, but WWII was largely a war against civilian populations. To give an idea: 20 million Russians, 20 million Chinese, 9 million Germans, 6 million Jews, 3 million Japanese. American and British losses, meanwhile, were less than one million combined. So you can see which countries took the brunt impact of that manufactured event.

Later in life, Dulles would admit Japan tried to surrender before the A-bombs were dropped, a largely symbolic event that unfortunately added immensely to the suffering and loss of completely innocent civilians.

Dulles Admits Japan Tried To Yield Before Hiroshima

By M. L. Mulford

Alka Dulles

If they needed a show of force, why the hell couldn't it have at least been a military target? Was it because shock and awe of such terrible human suffering was part of the strategy? I am reminded of a line in one of my favorite movies, *The Man Who Would Be King*, which tells the story of two Freemasons, veterans of the British Army, who find themselves stranded in India and after building a volunteer army they are marching into the first battle and Sean Connery says something like: "Make sure it is bloody. The bloodier the better." Well, that's the same attitude old money had regarding WWII, especially since most of that blood was spilled somewhere else.

Here's another key: spooks cannot be fired or retired. That's because when they start operations, they might be employed by an agency or corporation or anything, but once they become successful, they're running a secret network of operatives, all of whom carry out secret missions on a need-to-know basis. So as long as these agents get some operating costs and some mission bonuses, they'll keep functioning forever, even if their spook handler changes sides, because it's really all about the money and not the dogmas or even the patriotic causes.

And that's what happened in Germany because as soon as Hitler fell, his biggest spook went to straight to Dulles and changed sides and that Nazi spy network fell under operational control of Dulles.

Nazi spymaster Reinhard Gehlen made a secret surrender to Dulles.

Now JFK fired Dulles from heading the CIA and really humiliated him in the process. And I am sure Dulles plotted revenge, and obviously, he got it. Keep in mind that fired or not, Dulles retained operational control of the Nazi spook system and he had access to endless resources. But Dulles could not have acted unless he put together a core group of conspirators to assist in this mission. This group likely would have been kept to an absolute minimum, but had to include certain key individuals or success would not be guaranteed.

The key people who had to be on board the assassination with Allen Dulles were: J. Edgar Hoover, Lyndon Johnson, James Angleton, and some highly-placed people over at the Pentagon, because normal military support for protecting the president had to disappear, and the autopsy had to be performed at a military hospital to control the findings. But the actual hit squad that killed Kennedy ran straight through JM/Wave and ZR/Rifle.

Of course, the conspiracy could have gone much farther, into Sullivan & Cromwell, the most powerful law firm on Wall Street, and into the board room of the Federal Reserve, and perhaps even across the pond, where those masters of the black arts reside (and the price of gold and diamonds are fixed every day). The reality is, however, that the CIA takes its orders from the National Security Council, and the possibility exists that the council privately concluded JFK was a threat to national security.

A few years after the assassination, when Garrison's investigation rattled some windows at Langley, some major disinfo ops were undertaken and these likely would have been Angleton projects. The film experts in LA had worked on the Zapruder film and come up with a bootleg where it looked like the driver turned around to look at Kennedy (in response to the throat shot), and shot Kennedy himself before speeding off. Actually, glare off a bald head was magnified to look like a revolver in the driver's hands.

This rabbit hole is so Angleton because there already was tremendous confusion on whether the Secret Service was involved and whether the driver stopped in the kill zone to allow the shooters to triangulate and fire simultaneously. The team was on walkie-talkies and the most likely person giving the "go" would have been Shackley or Harvey, although Dealey Plaza was flooded with dozens of spooks that day, mostly from JM/Wave.

When Jackie Kennedy requested the driver also drive the hearse through the streets of Washington for the funeral, that led to speculation whether that mission was designed to remind one of the conspirators how beloved the man he'd helped kill was. The fact the driver was also one of the few outside the military allowed inside the autopsy room casts an ominous shadow on his possible role in the cover-up.

Suspiciously, the Lincoln slowed to a near-stop directly beside a man holding an umbrella by the curb, an umbrella that snapped open as the vehicle approached. A man holding a walkie-talkie stood nearby. At that moment, Roselli's opening shot went through the windshield inches from the driver's face, striking JFK in the throat, while Harvey fired a round that hit JFK in the back and another that hit Governor Connolly. The driver turned to look at JFK, while taking his foot off the gas. Was he reluctant to move into incoming fire, or had he been instructed to pause once the turkey shoot began? In that momentary pause, Charles Harrelson from the grassy knoll provided the *coup de grace*. The doctor at Parkland would pronounce the throat wound an entrance wound, but that determination got reversed after the body was seized at gunpoint by the Secret Service and taken to a Navy hospital, where an autopsy was overseen by unnamed admirals and generals, and all notes burned immediately afterwards.

Milton William Cooper.

The man who introduced the doctored Zapruder film to the world was a former naval intelligence officer who traveled around the country showing the clip, and later wrote the bible for a new generation of disinfo artists, and transformed the interpretation of the *Protocols*. His book became the most-read book in the American prison system. Like most disinfo, it was a confusing data dump jumble of documents and wild UFO assertions, although *Behold a Pale Horse* by William Cooper would bring back the *Protocols* to modern fame and mind ops, only this time, the world-wide council was revealed not as council of high-ranking Jews, but one of 33rd Degree Freemasons. Is it worth noting both J. Edgar Hoover and Chief Justice Earl Warren (who headed the official investigation) were Freemasons of the 33rd Degree? And that incoming President Johnson was also a member of this brotherhood? And so was Guy Bannister and others central to this story?

Now do you understand how complex these ops really are and how Dulles played such a scripted role? Yes, you can easily imagine this web extending straight to the Rockefellers and

Rothschilds, which is likely when it comes to the Rockefellers, but in reality, links across the pond have never been uncovered, leading to my suspicion the Rothschild meme is the rabbit hole. Cooper and all the rest of the disinfo artists, including the John Birch Society, keep pushing it so my instincts are screaming: don't look there for the head of the octopus, because that's obviously a mirror he is hiding behind, while he sips his cognac, puffs his cigar and pisses on all us slobs down here in the lower classes.

The Two Oswalds

Intelligence operations follow patterns and the most complex ones deploy diversions. It's what a stage magician does when needing to hide something. First, he attracts attention to the other hand.

On 9/11, for example, it appears nearly simultaneous to turning off the transponders, the hijacked planes crossed paths with other planes, which may have been done to swap the two out, or just to muddy their trail.

On September 28, when Oswald was supposedly in Mexico applying to visit Cuba, another Oswald was going around Dallas attracting attention in a way a spook like Oswald would not have done unless he was seeding important details into his legend, like the fake fight in New Orleans with anti-Castro Cubans. Oswald was seen a few times at the Sports Drome Range with a Mauser-like carbine with a scope. He spoke of how someone should shoot JFK, something not all that unpopular in the deep south (a junior high school class in Dallas erupted in applause upon hearing the news). Five weeks after Oswald appeared on the range, an assassination attempt on JFK planned for November 2nd in Chicago was thwarted by an undercover FBI informant identified only as "Lee."

42

Bizarrely, the suspect in the Chicago plot, Thomas Arthur Vallee, was an ex-Marine who'd been stationed at the two bases in Japan that housed U2 spy planes, same as Oswald, which is important because that's where some of the weirdest MK/Ultra mind control experiments were taken, likely to keep them off US soil. Vallee was a member of the John Birch Society and had trained with anti-Castro Cubans in Long Island. To make this digression even stranger, the same officers sent to arrest Vallee would later be accused of assassinating Black Panther Fred Hampton. In many respects Vallee was Oswald's doppleganger, only he was extreme right-wing while Oswald was pretending to be extreme left-wing. Today it seems rather obvious that "Lee" could have been Oswald. Another factor to keep in mind is there is no definitive evidence the real Oswald went to Mexico. The receptionist at the Cuban embassy he allegedly had an affair with later claimed the Oswald she slept with was short and blonde, perhaps the man photographed as Oswald outside the Cuban embassy.

Thomas Arthur Vallee.

It was a huge problem that no photo of Oswald entering the Cuban and/or Russian embassy could be found. And neither did a voice recording emerge. Hard evidence on anyone who walked into and/or called the Cuban or Russian embassies in Mexico

43

should have been easy to relocate, and if it did exist, it mysteriously disappeared. Of course, having a tape of someone impersonating Oswald on the phone would have been irrefutable proof of a larger conspiracy.

Man identified as Lee Harvey Oswald at Cuban embassy in Mexico.

Minutes after the assassination, Deputy Sheriff Roger Craig saw Oswald exit the Texas Schoolbook Depository and enter a light-green Rambler station wagon driven by a stocky Cuban (probably David Morales) before speeding off in the direction of Oak Cliff.

The CIA had a safe house in Oak Cliff stuffed with anti-Castro Cubans. Oswald had recently left his wife and child at Ruth Paine's in Irving, while renting a room in Oak Cliff over 12 miles away, perhaps because operations were heating up and becoming dangerous and he wanted to distance himself from his family and shield them from potential blowback. He'd spent the previous night at Paine's with Marina.

Officer J.D. Tippit was involved somehow in this operation and was aware of the danger because he told his son that morning, "No matter what happens today, just remember I love you." That was the last time his son saw his dad alive. It seems possible

Tippit may have been one of the few policemen who knew Oswald's true identity as a CIA/FBI undercover informant. He knew something big was happening that day, and he seems to have become panicked after he learned JFK was dead.

Tippit was driving frantically around Oak Cliff looking for someone, probably Oswald. A police car, perhaps Tippit's, pulled up in front of Oswald's rooming house right after he arrived home to retrieve his revolver. The car honked twice and then moved on, an obvious signal of some sort. Since two patrolmen had escorted the three tramps to anonymity earlier that day, however, I have to suspect those same two cops (who could never be identified) were probably the spooks dressed as cops who honked their horn, signaling it was time to go to the next stage of operations. I'll always wonder if those fake cops circled the block and then picked Oswald up at some prearranged location to deposit him at the Texas Theater, and then rushed off to 10th Street to plant Oswald's wallet at the Tippit murder scene.

J.D. Tippit.

Tippit was blocking an alley on East 10th Street seven blocks from the theater when he rolled down his passenger side window to speak to a pedestrian. It seems a police car may have already been in that alley nearby as police were on the scene almost immediately after the shooting. When Tippit exited his car and

45

came around to talk further, or perhaps to take the pedestrian into custody, the pedestrian shot him four times, including two point-blank shots to the head. Obviously, the shooter wanted insurance Tippit would not survive. Some sort of conversation took place and escalated from there and Tippit apparently didn't comprehend the danger he was in or he would not have left his vehicle without drawing his gun. It was a mob-style execution and not a gun fight.

Tippit murder scene.

The first cop on the scene picked up a wallet next to the spreading pool of Tippit's blood, and it had Lee Harvey Oswald's military ID. There were also four empty cartridges discovered at the scene as the shooter had emptied his revolver while walking away. How convenient! It's not often a murderer leaves his ID and spent cartridges like a trail of breadcrumbs to the magic kingdom. At this point there were zero suspects in JFK's assassination, but immediately after Tippit's murder, the story went out Lee Harvey Oswald was a suspect and had just murdered a policeman possibly as part of his getaway. Officer down! The response was staggering and almost every patrol car in Dallas converged on Oak Cliff. The focus was instantly concentrated entirely on Oswald and that focus never wavered.

By the time Tippit was shot, Oswald was already inside the Texas Theater. He'd been directed there by someone and was likely supposed to make contact with someone he didn't know. A theater is a logical location for a clandestine rendezvous because safe houses need to stay safe and we know there was a CIA safe house nearby. Oswald sat first in the balcony, but soon bought popcorn and moved down to the main floor, sitting for a few minutes right next to someone before moving on to another person. After he sat right next to a pregnant woman and had a brief conversation, she got up and moved to the balcony while Oswald moved again to sit next to another.

Whoever shot Tippit also came to the theater, but not before dumping a windbreaker under a vehicle behind a gas station. Suddenly, like those planes crossing as transponders go off, the two Oswalds came in close proximity for maybe the first time, and one of them had the entire Dallas police force on his tail. My best guess is the double came in a few minutes after Oswald, and he went unseen up into the balcony where the pregnant woman was now seated.

When the police arrived, they stopped the film, turned on the house lights and approached the audience from the stage and began inspecting everyone's IDs. When they got to Oswald, he allegedly jumped up and shouted, "It's all over now," and punched the nearest officer, who fell into the seats. He then pulled out his revolver and pointed it at the ceiling, or perhaps the floor, or maybe at the officer. Eyewitness testimony conflicts from this point. Witnesses claim to have heard the gun click, but no shots were fired. The arresting officer later somewhat absurdly claimed he'd placed his thumb on the hammer to prevent it from going off. Perhaps the revolver had a bent firing pin or was unloaded. Perhaps the speech was part of a script fed to him by his handler. Oswald was pummeled by many officers, handcuffed and taken out the front entrance to be greeted by an immense mob that included some media. He was not assassinated in the theater as might have been expected from flourishing a revolver shouting, "It's over." But then later on, some witnesses would say Oswald uttered those words while being led out of the building in handcuffs, and that's the problem: the most theatrical version possible often gets written in stone.

It appears the police may have continued inspecting IDs after Oswald was removed from the theater and may have gone up into the balcony where a man who looked somewhat like Oswald was also taken into custody and also handcuffed, only this person was taken out the back door and never showed up at the police station. And I say this because we have many witnesses to an Oswald coming out the front and one witness to an Oswald coming out the back. One of the oddest points of this case is we only know the names of a few people who were in that theater out of more than two dozen who bought tickets that day.

It's worth noting Oswald had a wallet on him when he was in the theater, leading to speculation about the mysterious wallet dropped at the scene of Tippit's murder, the wallet that put Oswald on the map in the first place. Sorta like the passport found at the World Trade Center that was disappeared from the story later on.

But perhaps the most bizarre saga of the two Oswalds is the story told by a refrigerator mechanic to the FBI four days after the assassination.

On November 20th, at 10:30 AM, Ralph Leon Yates was driving through Oak Cliff and stopped to pick up a hitchhiker near the Beckley Avenue, where Oswald lived. The hitchhiker carried a package wrapped in brown wrapping paper about 4 foot to 4½ feet long, saying it contained curtain rods. Yates mentioned the upcoming presidential visit and the hitchhiker responded by asking if he thought a person could assassinate the president and whether that might be best accomplished from the top of a building or out a window high up with a rifle. The man then asked about the President's parade route and whether that might be changed in the next few days. He also asked if Yates knew anyone named Jack Rubenstein.

Signed FBI statement by Ralph Leon Yates.

When Yates got to work, he told his coworker about this strange incident and later gave his story to the FBI on November 26, and again on December 10, January 3 and 4, concluding with a polygraph test, which he passed.

Strangely, Buell Frazier gave Oswald a ride from Ruth Paine's in Irving on the day of the assassination. This was a much longer trip, and, as usual, Oswald said nothing except to respond when Frazier asked what was in the 2-foot long package in the back seat. "Curtain rods," replied Oswald in his usual terse manner. "Remember, I told you about them?"

Since the packages were so different in size, yet had the same story, and since Oswald needed to arrive at work much earlier in the morning, one wonders if Yates drove the real Oswald to work, or his double. Was this a back-up plan for getting a rifle into the building? Or just a test run? Or just a way to salt the story of Oswald wanting to kill JFK? In any case, a paper bag the size Yates described was found inside the Texas School Book Depository the day of the assassination.

According to *JFK the Unspeakable*, Yates was soon committed to Woodlawn Hospital for an evaluation and then moved to Terrell State Hospital for eight years, and then placed in two different hospitals for another three years. He never abandoned his story about giving Oswald a ride to work with the murder weapon, no matter how many electric shocks he got. The Warren Commission dismissed his story as a fantasy, probably because they had a better version for how the rifle got into the building from Frazier, although Frazier never believed the two-foot long package he saw on the back seat of his car was a 36-inch carbine, no matter how long they interrogated him, and Frazier was badgered for nearly 12 hours, and only released after he demanded (and passed) a lie detector test, which was pretty savy for a 19-year-old kid. To this day, Frazier believes Oswald was framed.

Yates, on the other hand, died in a psyche ward of congestive heart failure at age 39.

Since proof of Oswald cohorts prior to the event is proof of a larger conspiracy, it's amazing that proof actually got published by the Warren Commission and somehow swept under the rug for decades.

A month before the assassination, the Odio sisters living in Dallas were visited by three men, two of whom claimed to be members of her father's organization, the Junta Revolucionanria, a left-wing organization that was anti-capitalist but also anti-Castro. They claimed the white man with them, introduced as Leon Oswald, had just volunteered to go kill Castro. Having been warned by her father (who was in jail in Cuba) about strange men bearing tales of intrigue, Sylvia Odio refused to get involved with any illegal activities or even admit the men inside her apartment.

The next day, the tall leader of the group (who called himself Leopoldo), phoned to say: "Leon is a former Marine and an expert marksman. He says we Cubans don't have guts because we should have killed Kennedy after the Bay of Pigs."

A few weeks later, Odio saw Oswald on TV and instantly recognized him. She called the police and volunteered her story, and it became part of the public record. One of the more fascinating aspects of her testimony is it placed Oswald inside an infiltration operation cloaked as an assassination, which means obtaining a Mauser-like weapon with scope, and attracting attention to himself at the local firing range could have been staged as part of that operation, as well as his attempt to get a visa to Cuba. It should be obvious Oswald was a highly-trained spook, but he was certainly not part of any double zero crew (the guys who pull triggers). And he couldn't have been at the firing range, and sitting inside the Cuban embassy sweet-talking Silvia Duran at the same time, although he apparently was. And eerily, an antagonistic attitude towards JFK for a Bay of Pigs fiasco was part of the script according to Leopoldo, which might explain Oswald making similar hostile comments on the firing range.

Mark Lane was one of the few skeptics allowed to testify at the Warren Commission, and could have easily shredded the official story had he brought attention to the Odio affidavit and a few others. Instead Lane launched into a bizarre attack on the backyard photo of Oswald as being a fake and also claimed the rifle in the photo was not the same as the rifle as found at the Texas School Book Depository because it had no scope. Lane had sought to examine the rifle in custody and complained bitterly about not being allowed to.

I find this fascinating because Lane was certainly aware of Deputy Sheriff Roger Craig's testimony stating the rifle found on the sixth floor was a German Mauser. Why would he need to examine the highly inferior Carcano when obviously it was a swap-out? Before Lane appeared in Dallas, newspaperman Penn Jones was already on the scene, and highly suspicious of a military intelligence operation. Jones, however, was elbowed out of the spotlight and replaced by Lane. Apparently, seizing the center of gravity on a conspiracy is standard ops for counterintelligence, and they do it with every major conspiracy they want to cover-up.

Even more suspicious, Oswald's wife admitted taking the backyard photo, and a different take from same the photoshoot signed by Oswald had been presented to George de Mohrenschildt, a man who started out spooking for the Nazis. So why would Lane make this photo the crux of a conspiracy case, unless he was intentionally planting a rabbit hole with a time bomb?

And the rabbit holes just keep going deeper because in 2003, Robert Vinson came forward and signed an affidavit attesting to hearing an Air Force colonel on November 21 warning someone over the phone that JFK better not show up in Dallas the next day. Vinson claims to have boarded a military cargo flight to Denver the following day that detoured to pick up two men in Dallas, one of whom he later realized was a dead ringer for Oswald. Vinson also admitted to working for the CIA. He waited decades to come forward and only did so because a lawyer told him a new secrecy act released him from keeping silent.

And here's the problem. The assassination was meticulously planned on so many levels and with so many layers that it is inconceivable a cargo plane would have been diverted at the last second for a crucial escape. In fact, the escape is always the most well-planned part of any covert operation. Just as the original JFK research field was dominated by spooks like Mark Lane and Mary Ferrell, both of whom failed to expose the plotters, a new generation has come forth spinning tales that sometime seem designed to muddy the waters or make someone rich and famous.

Brigade 2506 reunion.

Over the decades it's been pretty well established that Leopoldo was the Intelligence Chief for Brigade 2506, the group massacred at the Bay of Pigs, a man really named Bernardo De Torres (note he is fourth from the right and tallest in the preceding photo). De Torres had been captured and jailed and just recently released and returned to the States when he met the Odios.

De Torres later told his daughter he was in Florida the day of the assassination and had launched his own private investigation into the incident but had to abruptly halt it after discovering the truth. He showed up and volunteered as an investigator for Jim Garrison after Garrison launched the only real government investigation. Yet every promising lead De Torres unveiled to Garrison led into a dead-end. De Torres' primary aim seemed to be casting suspicion on Castro as Kennedy's real killer. Eventually Garrison became convinced De Torres was secretly working with the CIA to disrupt the investigation.

After being dismissed from Garrison's inner circle, De Torres immediately went to work for super spook Mitch Werbell as an arms dealer in Latin America, and, according to some, became a major player in the narcotics trade. Gaeton Fonzi would establish that De Torres was one of the 25-odd spooks in and around Dealey Plaza that day and was posing as a photographer during the event. Apparently, De Torres kept those photos in a safe deposit box as his own personal life insurance policy.

Buell Frazier

Buel Frazier was only 19 when he met Lee Harvey Oswald. They both worked at the Texas School Book Depository for minimum wage ($1.50) and Frazier sometimes drove Oswald the 15 miles to work if his broken-down Chevy was functional. The day of the assassination Oswald appeared with a two-foot-long package and told Frazier they were curtain rods. When they arrived at work, Oswald carried the package between his palm and armpit.

Frazier never swallowed the story that short package was actually a 36-inch Mannlicher-Carcano rifle. Nor did he swallow the story that soft-spoken, highly intelligent Lee Oswald shot JFK that day.

A much different, longer package from the one Frazier had seen that morning was produced for the media. Enormous efforts were made to connect Oswald to the murder weapon, and some of this activity seems to have involved fabricating evidence as it went along, which is why there was so much revision. The problem with the enormous bag shown to the media is it was put together with tape from the book depository, indicating it wasn't the bag Oswald carried because his bag had been manufactured off-site.

I have no doubt Oswald was instructed to bring a package to work that day because he was seen departing the scene in a green Rambler station wagon driven by David Morales, or someone who looked much like Morales. Two others might have been hiding on the floorboards inside, one of whom could have been Ted Shackley. I wonder if Bill Harvey was the third seen entering that Rambler right after the murder that afternoon. Certainly that trio worked on a number of murderous missions over the years.

Buell Frazier on the day of the assassination.

Frazier was put through a 12-hour hostile interrogation and told at one point that Oswald had named him as a co-conspirator. He demanded and eventually got a lie detector test, which he easily passed. However, the hostility of the police towards his belief in Oswald's innocence caused Frazier to lie very low for a long time.

He was pressured to change his story and also change the length of the bag by the Warren Commission, but never wavered. The Commission eventually rejected his story and concluded his memory was not accurate.

The Mauser

Deputy Sheriff Roger Craig is one of the greatest unsung heroes who sought justice after JFK's murder in Dallas. Craig arrived at Dealey Plaza seconds after the shooting and raced to the picket fence at the top of the knoll, closely following the motorcycle cop who'd ditched his bike to run up the hill. The scene behind the fence was chaotic because a large number of people had already gathered. There were footprints and cigarette butts near where many witnesses saw a plume of smoke appear as the shots rang out.

Craig noticed a woman attempting to drive out of the parking lot and stopped her, taking her into custody for questioning. Deputy Sheriff Lewis appeared and took her off his hands.

Craig then crossed Elm Street and began interviewing witnesses. Arnold Rowland and his wife said they saw a man with a rifle in a Texas School Book Depository window overlooking the plaza before the presidential limo arrived. They hadn't said anything because they assumed he was a secret service agent. Deputy Lewis appeared again and took the Rowlands off his hands.

Suddenly, a shrill whistle sounded and Craig noticed a man in his twenties run down the knoll from the direction of the depository. A green Rambler station wagon slowed and the man jumped inside. Craig wanted to detain this vehicle, but traffic was intense and he failed to cross in time. When he did make it across, Craig went to the depository steps and was greeted by a man claiming to be a Secret Service agent. Craig began talking about the suspicious Rambler, but the agent seemed little interested. Craig's boss, Sheriff Decker appeared and told Craig the suspect had left the scene and someone should search inside the depository.

Roger Craig.

Upon arriving at the sixth floor, Craig quickly located three spent cartridges by the southeast corner window, all lined up as if carefully set in place, something he found highly suspicious. One cartridge had a strange crimp. A rifle was soon located stashed in a pile of cardboard boxes. Stamped on the barrel was "7.65 Mauser." Captain Fritz, chief of homicide for Dallas, arrived and took possession. That night the murder weapon used to kill JFK was described on all three networks as a German Mauser. The Mauser is a short-barreled carbine invented for use by cavalry officers. Carbines are not typically a weapon of choice among professional snipers due to limited range and low-bullet velocity. They are, however, slightly easier to conceal than long barrel rifles, especially when broken in two segments. The Italians made a cheap imitation of the Mauser, the 6.5 Mannlicher-Carcano, which was dumped on the market after WWII for around $5 each wholesale.

Problem is the cartridges on the floor were 6.5 Carcanos, which meant the German rifle and Italian cartridges didn't match.

"I arrived at Capt. Fritz office shortly after 4:30 PM," wrote Craig later. "I was met by Agent Bookhout from the F.B.I., who took my name and place of employment. The door to Capt. Fritz' personal office was open and the blinds on the windows were closed, so that one had to look through the doorway in order to see into the room. I looked through the open door at the request of Capt. Fritz and identified the man who I saw running down the grassy knoll and enter the Rambler station wagon—and it WAS Lee Harvey Oswald. Fritz and I entered his private office together. He told Oswald, this man (pointing to me) saw you leave. At which time the suspect replied, I told you people I did. Fritz, apparently trying to console Oswald, said, take it easy, son—we're just trying to find out what happened. Fritz then said, what about the car? Oswald replied, leaning forward on Fritz' desk, that station wagon belongs to Mrs. Paine—don't try to drag her into this. Sitting back in his chair, Oswald said very disgustedly and very low, everybody will know who I am now."

Because he was a Dallas police officer, it was impossible for the Warren Commission to completely ignore Craig. However, when the Commission report was released significant changes were made to his testimony. Meanwhile, Craig was ordered never to talk about the case with anyone in the media. After being caught talking to someone, he was fired.

Like other important witnesses, Craig was shot at, driven off the road, and hounded at almost every twist and turn of his remaining short life. As a key witness to the assassination, he'd assumed he'd become famous someday, but instead was quickly flushed down a rabbit hole. Many early gatekeepers like Mary Ferrell worked hard to discredit him, which, in hindsight is probably the best indication of how important he really was. Mary Ferrell was a lawyer for Mobile who made the assassination her life's obsession. She never really managed to connect the dots on the case, even though the most obvious trail led straight into JM/Wave, and to Harvey, Shackley and Morales. Craig sadly died of a gunshot to the chest in 1975. Self-inflicted so they say and it could be true because he was a completely broken man whose autobiography had been universally rejected by the publishing world.

During the Garrison trial against the CIA, Craig was astounded to see images of the alleged Secret Service agent he ran into on the depository steps. His real name was Edgar Eugene Bradley, and he was a rightwing preacher from North Hollywood, California, and part-time assistant to Carl McIntire, the fundamentalist minister who had founded the American Counsel of Christian Churches.

Richard Randolph Carr

Although Dealey Plaza was loaded with important witnesses who picked up fragmentary clues on who killed JFK, the most important ones were culled out and never interviewed by the Warren Commission. In hindsight it appears the more important an eyewitness testimony was, the more likely it would be flushed down a rabbit hole early in the game.

Several people claimed to have seen men acting strangely on the fifth and sixth floors of the Texas School Book Depository that tragic afternoon, and Richard Carr was one of the most important. He was interviewed by the FBI, although the report filed by the agents left out important details. This was not Carr's fault, obviously, but evidence of FBI manipulation of the case. During his FBI interview Carr was told something along the lines of: "If you didn't see Lee Harvey Oswald with a gun on the sixth floor, you didn't see anything and better keep your mouth shut." So Carr did exactly that until the Garrison investigation emerged several years later.

Richard Randolph Carr.

Although Garrison wisely tried to launch his investigation in secret, it was immediately exposed and denigrated by the media. Immense efforts were made to shut it down, and when that didn't succeed they surrounded Garrison with spooks on all sides and snowed him under with useless leads to nowhere.

Although some honest journalists appeared early on the scene, there were eight or nine secret agents sowing disinfo for every honest researcher like Penn Jones. The center of gravity was quickly handed off to suspicious characters, two of whom were lawyers: Mark Lane (former army intelligence) and Mary Ferrell (attorney for Mobil). While the FBI and CIA were busy destroying and hiding evidence, fake researchers were snowing the case under with inconsequential details and rabbit holes.

One of the most effective items floated out was *Nomenclature of an Assassination Cabal* by William Torbitt, a pseudonym for a Texas lawyer with intelligence connections. Like most disinfo, it established its bona fides by revealing something real: the participation of a Swiss Corporation named Permidex in helping fund the assassination. From there, it went on to blame the FBI's Division 5 working with NASA and others. Torbitt implicated many people, most of whom did not play any role. Yet for decades, many researchers took it as unbridled truth, while in reality, it was designed to steer researchers away from the obvious culprit needing investigation: the CIA.

Carr's original FBI report documents the two individuals he saw on the sixth floor during the shooting. As he moved closer to the scene, he saw three men flee in a Rambler station wagon, easily recognized by a unique mini-luggage rack. Carr began receiving death threats telling him to leave Texas. He moved to Montana, where Garrison tracked him down.

When Carr testified in New Orleans, many important details were added to the sketchy FBI statement. He managed to miraculously survive two murder attempts, one by gun and one by knife. When stabbed in Atlanta, he managed to kill one of his two assailants, a remarkable feat. He died in West Virginia on August 4, 1996, and was never located by the Congressional investigation, although they did make note of his contributions to the case. The part I find most fascinating is his description of the team on the sixth floor. One was a stocky Cuban or Spanish man, and the other a taller man with distinctive thick-framed glasses.

Over the decades, the secret of Permidex was finally uncovered. The company was a cut-out deployed by the Italian CIA officers. At the time of JFK assassination, the head of the CIA in Italy was William Harvey. Harvey was supposed to have been fired after his anti-Cuban plans were rejected during a confrontational meeting in the White House. Instead, Angleton and Dulles moved Harvey to Rome, where he began assisting their secret plans to eliminate JFK.

Theodore Shackley pioneered the thick-frame glasses look.

Six weeks before the assassination, documents about Oswald began floating through the intelligence community. Strangely, the memos made no reference to Oswald's recent altercations in New Orleans or participation in pro-Castro organizations, only his defection-to and return-from the Soviet Union. In fact, they went further indicating Oswald's Soviet sojourn had matured his political views. Many signing off on this memo had to realize the information was fraudulent. The appearance of the suspicious Oswald memo indicates the beginning of Oswald's entanglement in the JFK assassination plot.

Morales became a suspect in the RFK assassination before retiring in 1975. He returned to his native Arizona, and died of a heart attack in 1978. A Congressional investigator tracked Morales to Wilcox, Arizona shortly after his death, and talked to his friend Ruben Carbajal and a business associate of Morales' named Bob Walton. Walton revealed Morales once went into a tirade about Kennedy at a bar after several drinks, and finished by saying

"Well, we took care of that son of a bitch, didn't we?" Carbajal, who had been present at this confession, provided corroboration.

David Morales.

Harvey, Shackley and Morales were named as participating in the event by Howard Hunt's deathbed confession. It's unfortunate they were never seriously investigated, nor were they ever put in a room with Carr to find out if they were the mystery trio he saw fleeing the scene.

Revilo P. Oliver

Once you identify the principle polemicists salting the intel-sponsored propaganda, you're halfway to enlightenment; and once you identify the major memes those polemicists are salting, you can easily ID a lot more spooks and avoid their rabbit holes to nowhere. Anyone supporting obviously fake memes is either a spook or hoodwinked true believer and there is no other option. Spooks and true believers can't be trusted, so divide conspiracy research into two categories, trusted and not trusted, and learn from both categories. With practice and a keen eye for detail, you'll soon be learning more from the disinfo than the authentic intel (mostly because there's a lot more noise than signal). But you must avoid falling into the traps, what I call the rabbit holes, the biggest of which is racism in any form. The most powerful forces promoting ethnic cleansing are spook-driven, manufactured to assist the war-for-profit scenarios with their divide-and-conquer propaganda, something always easily identified.

Revilo P. Oliver.

The post-WWI generation was turned against Jews in many ways and on many levels, but mostly through Earnest Hemingway and F. Scott Fitzgerald, both of whom demeaned the culture whenever possible. These were the two most influential novelists when novels were an influence. At the time, Jews were not integrated into high society, not allowed to join the country clubs or fraternities of the oligarchy. Instead, rich Jews had their own aristocracy centered on families holding stock in the Federal Reserve, the ones who also owned some of the biggest investment banks, the ones linked to names like Rothschild and Warburg. This division between these two powerful oligarchies along the Eastern seaboard was intentional and in place prior to the Civil War. They are still separate in some quarters.

I suspect Oliver worked for OSS during WWII. He was a brilliant intellectual and mastered a dozen languages, and was considered an expert in the origins of religion. He taught at the University of Illinois, where I grew up, evolving into a major player on the national stage. He had a hand in creating the John Birch Society and the National Alliance, now known as the National Vanguard. Funny, how nobody writes or talks about Oliver today, except his supporters, even though his role as a spook propagandist should be obvious with hindsight.

Soon after JFK's assassination, Oliver published a dissenting opinion claiming JFK was a communist who'd been murdered by the communists because he'd decided to "go American." He claimed Lee Harvey Oswald had been trained by the KGB, and the Warren Commission had been preordained to claim Oswald was a lone assassin. This was published after the commission was announced, long before the 888-page report appeared. Oliver's theory was peppered with distortions and outright fabrications, as well as some amazing secret truths, evidence of inside sources. The government, especially the State Department, was heavily penetrated by a secret communist conspiracy run by Jews, claimed Oliver, and as evidence he cited the impossibility of a Marine formerly posted at our most secret base in Japan defecting to Russia, and then freely returning to America, and yet not monitored by the FBI. This could only happen if the State Department was infested with cooperating communist conspirators claimed Oliver, ignoring the more obvious explanation Oswald was an American spook who was returning from a failed penetration operation in Russia.

"The identification of the murderer was a near-miracle. If not the result of divine intervention, it was the result of a series of coincidences of the same order as might enable a bum with a dollar in his pocket to enter a casino in Reno and emerge with a thousand," noted Oliver, in another one of his many spot-on assessments. This miraculous identification and capture of Oswald began with the murder of Officer J.D. Tippit. Oswald's wallet was discovered at the scene, along with four spent cartridges from his revolver. Strange Oliver could recognize the anomaly of Oswald's strangely trouble-free re-entry into the USA after supposedly defecting to the enemy, but missed this highly improbable wallet, especially considering Oswald was captured an hour later with a wallet in his pocket. Which means the wallet at the scene was planted. There's also the witnesses to the Tippet slaying who claim Oswald was not the man they saw fleeing the crime. The only other option is believing the official story Oswald murdered Tippet, then calmly emptied his revolver, tossed his wallet on the ground and then fled the scene, which is the version Oliver opted for in this instance.

"Americans known to be opponents of the Conspiracy, including General Walker, prominent members of the John Birch Society, and leaders of other conservative organizations, began to receive threats of death by telephone from creatures who somehow knew that Kennedy was dead *before* he reached the hospital," wrote Oliver. I believe this detail is also spot-on in that Texas John Birch supporters put up the $150,000 to pay the three shooters and were among the first notified of the mission's success, but salting that observation with the lie these calls included death threats to the paymasters is an obvious misdirection that recalls Edwin Stanton's efforts to claim he was a target of the Lincoln assassination conspiracy, and not one of the instigators himself.

Oliver was especially harsh on the then director of the Council on Foreign Relations, the recently-fired former CIA head, Allen W. Dulles. "Dulles was the head of an American spy ring in Switzerland during the Second World War and is said to have done a fairly good job," began Oliver, "although it was believed at the time that his organization was infested with double agents who were really in the employ of the Soviet — and even more serious implications can be drawn from the testimony given in Karlsruhe last July by Heinz Felfe, a Soviet agent who had been Mr. Dulles' German counterpart and supposed competitor in Switzerland." Yes, Dulles was head of OSS in Europe and was posted in Switzerland, and recruited the bulk of the Nazi spy network into the CIA in a secret surrender with Malta Knight Reinhardt Gehlen, who was later rewarded by becoming head of the West German secret services, but Felfe was a minor figure when posted in Switzerland compared with Dulles, and just one of many spooks accepting pay from all comers.

"One writer has recently suggested that it was the C.I.A. that arranged the assassination of Kennedy; I know of no evidence to support that opinion, but obviously Mr. Dulles' creation is open to suspicion. Perhaps that is why he is a member of the "special commission," wrote Oliver in a brief and startling moment of spot-on clarity that was instantly jettisoned.

Oliver claimed the commission would paint "Comrade Oswald as a poor, lone critter who done it all alone. Probably 'psychiatrists' will be produced to prove he done it 'cause, at the age of six months, he had to wait an extra five minutes for his bottle." Strange that Oswald was likely worked on by CIA psychiatrists while a teen in New York, prior to his being hypnotized by David Ferry while a member of Ferry's Civil Air Patrol in New Orleans. The fact he knew the outcome before the investigation began was yet another spot-on.

Oliver was called before the Warren Commission to testify, and I imagine that was a scripted encounter. Mark Lane was another one of the few independent investigators allowed to present evidence directly to the Commission. It took me decades to realize Lane's testimony was likely scripted as well, for he was also a former OSS officer, and was likely guided into a role as the premier debunker of the official story. He soon tainted himself by embracing Willis Carto's holocaust denial movement. Isn't it strange that both Oliver and Lane were on polar opposites of the political divide, one far left the other far right, and yet both believed in a Jewish conspiracy running the world.

If you want to find a contemporary salter of disinfo, check out Jan Irvin, who treads in Oliver's footsteps with lies and distortions. Irvin produces propaganda supporting the theory the hippies were created by the CIA, and that Tim Leary, Ken Kesey and me are employees of that agency, and not its critics. Since I'm on the inside of this particular conspiracy theory, it's impossible for me to ignore Irvin is making shit up. So I put him in the "not trusted" category. And wouldn't you know, he also believes Jews are running the system through some secret satanic cult based on the teachings of Aleister Crowley, which just confirms my suspicions intel is exploiting Crowley for propaganda. But they do the same thing with their phony UFO evidence they are constantly manufacturing.

My advice: avoid any variation on any rabbit holes resembling: Communists are running the world; Jews are running the world; Satanists are running the world, or the CIA created the hippies.

Vince Salandria

The Warren Commission had problems right out-of-the-gate, and the biggest became known as the single bullet theory. Even though the wounds were tampered with and notes of the autopsy immediately burned, the official report had considerable difficulty explaining how one pristine bullet found on the stretcher at Parkland Hospital caused seven wounds in two men. The solution was invented by a young Philadelphia DA, who would soon rise to great heights in American politics. His name was Arlen Specter.

In 1964, Vince Salandria was a history teacher at Bartram High School with a law degree who did legal work on the side when Specter was invited by the local bar association to give a talk concerning his work for the Commission. Specter spoke in front of an audience of 150, and then asked if anyone had a question. Salandria stood up. "Your single bullet theory is a fraud, a magic bullet theory," he began. "How could anyone support such a blatant absurdity?"

"Have you read the report?" smirked Specter.

"Yes, I have," replied Salandria, "all eight hundred and eighty-eight pages."

Vince Salandria

Specter was visibly taken aback. He'd not been expecting opposition on this dog-and-pony show, much less from someone so well-armed with facts. After JFK was assassinated Salandria told himself if Lee Harvey Oswald was killed before any trial took place, it would mean the CIA was behind the coup. When that happened, he drove to Dallas to investigate and interview witnesses. He met with Oswald's mother, who told him her son

70

was in the CIA, and she was very proud of that fact. In the Warren Commission Report, Specter had successfully painted Oswald's mom as a lunatic. He tried sparring with Salandria but after losing every parry, Specter asked for a new question and moved on, his credibility somewhat shaken. It was a scary moment when the entire facade threatened to come down, and Specter would never forget it..

Salandria went home in an inspirational fever created by the audience's reaction to his comments and composed the first critique of Specter's theory, and soon had it published it in Philadelphia's *Legal Intelligencer,* becoming an instant star inside a growing band of citizen researchers disputing the official story of JFK's murder. These debunkers were virtually shunned because so few believed the CIA would kill its own President.

A few years ago a professor in Florida did his own digging around, and uncovered this document through the FOIA that revealed the CIA invented the term "conspiracy theorist" as a derogatory term to be deployed while dismissing critics of the Warren Commission Report. The document outlined a variety of strategies for debunking the debunkers.

In order to cement the fallacy of the conspiracy theorists they needed to invent some really nutty conspiracy theories, so what happened next is a string of whistle-blowers introduced mind-blowing new evidence in JFK's assassination, and then began pursuing completely different conspiracy theories, often involving aliens, theories that could easily be swatted away, thus tainting and negating any JFK revelations.

Two of the original memes they introduced were "dead people are alive" and "living people are dead." I don't know which came first, Elvis or Paul, but both were extensively mined for this counterintelligence propaganda operation.

71

The photo that launched the Elvis meme was accompanied by the release of documents from Elvis' DEA and FBI files. Not only had Elvis traveled to Washington DC seeking credentials as a Special Agent in the war on drugs, one of his airplanes had been investigated during a drug investigation. Elvis had zero to do with illegal drug-running, but was a heavy user of legally-prescribed narcotics. Both the "Elvis is alive" and "Paul is dead" memes were promoted extensively by the *Weekly World News*, which I strongly suspect was deployed as a counterintelligence propaganda tool for dumbing down America, a role the entire media complex seems to be embracing these days.

More recently people inside the Air Force have confessed to planting fake evidence of alien visitations in the UFO community. And wouldn't you know a lot of early JFK researchers ended up promoting the "aliens are here" meme. Most of this disinfo came in the form of forged "top secret" documents that never existed in the real world, and since intel deals with these sorts of memos every day, they know how to forge them and make them look really good.

The growth and spread of phony intel propaganda memes over the decades dwarfs the efforts of real citizen researchers, the noise to signal ratio is immense, and the landscape now includes "we never landed on the moon," chemtrails, "no one got killed at Sandy Hook," "no planes were used in 9/11," and many, many more. As Goebbels noted, "tell a big lie, and stick to it." Only I believe he was talking about the British MI6 propaganda and not his own.

Strangely, at the end of his long career, Specter invited Salandria to lunch at the Oyster Bar in Philadelphia. Salandria was surprised by this invitation and ended up doing most of the talking. He'd ended up losing his teaching job for promoting conspiracy theory among his students. Perhaps Specter was pumping him for the state-of-the-art in JFK research, or maybe he was trying to improve his karma. Specter's last words were along the lines of perhaps he hadn't been fraudulent after all, but merely incompetent. "You're not that incompetent," replied Salandria.

Abraham Bolden and Thomas Vallee

Twenty-three days before the assassination of JFK in Dallas, Oswald walked into the FBI offices in Dallas and delivered a handwritten note for agent James Hosty. After JFK's murder, Hosty was ordered to destroy this note and it took many years to uncover what that note might have said and why it had to be destroyed immediately after the assassination. The official story given by Hosty was it contained "some sort of threat," but that later changed to the more ludicrous: "stay away from my wife."

In fact, the note likely claimed that a four-man assassination team had assembled in Chicago for the purpose of assassinating JFK on his way to Soldier Field for the annual Army-Air Force football game, an assassination scheduled to take place on November 2. We only know this because a Chicago-based secret service agent named Abraham Bolden was asked to investigate the allegation and two men were placed under surveillance and soon picked up later that day and brought to the Secret Service offices in Chicago, and then mysteriously released without being conclusively identified for the record. These two suspects may have been Roselli and Harvey, or maybe they were the guys not picked up, but it's clear the two suspects were spooks just from the way the investigation unfolded without arrest or noticeable investigative paperwork. Bolden only knew the tip had come from an FBI informant named "Lee." And he later turned whistleblower and paid the price.

By strange coincidence, another chance encounter had put the Chicago assassination mission in jeopardy, as the patsy had inadvertently prematurely come under investigation. Remarkably, that patsy bore an amazing resemblance to Oswald. His name was Thomas Arthur Vallee and he'd been overheard making threats against JFK at a diner, where he was confronted by an undercover officer who reported the incident to Chicago Secret Service.

Abraham Bolden.

Two Chicago police officers were sent to investigate Vallee, and they both ended up rising rapidly through the ranks: Daniel Groth and Peter Schurla. Right around the time JFK cancelled his

Chicago trip (just an hour before he was due to take off), Groth and Schurla went to see Vallee. He told them he'd been assigned to a U2 base in Japan (just like Oswald) and had a small arsenal and hundreds of rounds of ammunition. He was a devoted member of the John Birch Society, which means he likely believed JFK was a communist agent bent on destruction of the United States.

Photos of his vehicle revealed that Vallee had a license plate that was protected by national security. He was also a certified mental patient with a metal plate in his head and a history of emotional breakdowns.

Since there was also another plot based in Miami one wonders if an ex-Marine from a U2 base in Japan was also being moved into a tall office building overlooking a parade route. Because that's what happened to both Oswald and Vallee during the month of November. More likely, however, the Miami plot would have involved a Cuban patsy, and there were so many to choose from. But the locations of Chicago, Miami and Dallas are telling because that's where Dulles and Angleton felt they had the best control over the situation.

And what about Bolden? Well, he tried to testify before the Warren Commission. But before that happened, he was set up on a bribery and attempted murder charge. Bolden served 39 months in jail and two-and-a-half years in probation. Afterwards he would write a book asserting the assassination was a conspiracy and the Secret Service was a racist and corrupt organization that overlooked boozing and broads on duty for the elite insiders. And it also later emerged the key figure in setting Bolden up to prevent his Warren Commission testimony was none other than Roselli, one of JFK's known assassins. Roselli's stool pigeon, who testified against Bolden, later recanted and claimed all accusations had been coerced in exchange for a lenient sentence on an unrelated gambling charge.

Oswald's wallets

Patterns are the key element in unmasking deep state operations because counterintelligence employs time-tested strategies to assure the success of their missions. One tool in their arsenal is planting evidence at the scene pointing toward a designated patsy. Along these lines you'll find the pristine bullet left on JFK's stretcher at Parkland Hospital, a driver's license planted in a stolen car following the Charlie Hebdo assassinations in France and a passport allegedly found in the rubble of the World Trade Towers, although that passport story seemed to vaporize indicating it was a rabbit hole with a time bomb attached.

Most Americans aren't aware Oswald became a suspect only after a wallet was planted at the scene of the murder of officer J.D. Tippit. This wallet became the key evidence deployed to prove Oswald murdered Tippet. The wallet contained Oswald's military ID card, was well as an Alek James Hidell ID card, and since the alleged murder weapon had been ordered by someone using that name, that ID became the key evidence to convince many Oswald murdered JFK as well. The wallet was discovered 40 minutes after JFK's assassination and within minutes of its discovery, Oswald was ID'd as the primary suspect in JFK's death. He was arrested 45 minutes after Tippet's murder.

There was one glaring problem with this timeline, however. When Oswald was arrested at the movie theater, he refused to give a name to the arresting officers, and instead punched an officer and then flourished a revolver, which was taken away from him. They removed his wallet at the theater in order to ID him. Both wallets were duly entered into a chain of custody, yet only one wallet was sent to Washington DC, while the other remained buried in Dallas at the police station and would not be uncovered for decades.

A month before the assassination, Oswald began appearing at the local rifle range, practicing with a Mauser-like carbine with scope, shooting at other people's targets, talking about how someone shot shoot JFK, something not that uncommon in the deep south.

Oswald was also supposed to be in Mexico City at the same time, applying for a visa to Cuba. Only the CIA could never produce any evidence the real Oswald was in Cuba. And since he was seen at the range at the same time, we must assume the Mexico trip was undertaken by someone assuming his identity.

While none of the initial witnesses on the scene mentioned a wallet (and one of them used Tippet's radio to call for help), after the ambulance and police and a news crew showed up, some anonymous person handed a wallet to the arriving officer saying it had been "left at the scene." Also found were four spent cartridges from Oswald's revolver. In other words, we are expected to believe Oswald shot Tippet, then calmly emptied his revolver cartridges and tossed his wallet on the ground so police would have the evidence needed to convict him, like a trail of breadcrumbs leading to the Oz.

Meanwhile, when Oswald was booked his hands and cheek showed no evidence of firing a weapon and it was a Mauser that was initially discovered inside the School Book Depository, not the Mannlicher Carcano ordered by Alek Hidell.

When the Carcano was tested for fingerprints, it had none, leading to speculation Oswald had been using the Mauser at the range. Fortunately, when tested later, after Oswald's murder, a palm print matching Oswald's was found on the Carcano, leading to speculation the print had been taken off the corpse.

Babushka Lady

The overdressed and remarkably calm Babushka Lady stands out as one of the most mysterious figures in JFK's assassination. She was methodically panning the kill zone before the shooting started and continued to document as events unfolded. I have to wonder if she was James Angleton's eyes and ears on the ground in Dallas that day, so well-positioned was she to capture the murder. Whatever film she shot has never seen the light of day, although it likely remains deep in some repository at the House of Langley.

Penn Jones was a veteran who owned a newspaper in a Texas town with a population 1,500. He was the first honest journalist to start investigating the assassination, and immediately suspected a military intelligence operation. Mark Lane, a former Army intelligence officer, quickly arrived on the scene, and elbowed Jones off the national stage. Meanwhile, Lane's book was a confusing mess of details that failed to expose the plot's center of gravity at JM/Wave, the largest CIA base outside of Langley.

The spooks keep at least two steps ahead of any media coverage, and since they control most of the media, this is easily arranged. Jones was blacklisted from the national media, but he did pick up a young admirer named J. Gary Shaw, who claimed to have discovered the Babushka Lady.

Here's what Babushka Lady looked like, and keep in mind it's 67 degrees in Dallas and undoubtedly feels hotter in the full sun, yet she wears an enormous trench coat, fully buttoned. She appears attractive and middle-aged in her one close-up portrait. One must never discount the power of honey-traps in spook world and she could have been a player and certainly exudes self-confidence.

According to Shaw, Babushka Lady was really 18-year-old Beverly Oliver, an exotic dancer at a club across the street from Jack Ruby's Carousel Club. Shaw and Oliver were members of the same Christian sect, and Oliver was filmed singing *Amazing Grace* for a documentary on the assassination featuring Shaw. Oliver took center-stage at a few JFK assassination conferences but her story grew more convoluted and less believable as time went on.

The art of hypnosis being what it is, it's impossible to determine how many JFK assassination whistleblowers are real, fake, or delusional. Like all deep political events, however, this landscape is dotted with frauds and rabbit holes, and while I concede Beverly bears a resemblance to Babushka Lady, I can't believe that photo above was her at age 18, nor would an 18-year-old dress like that on a hot day in Dallas.

Most important, nothing in Beverly's story explained how she'd remained so calm when such incredible turbulence was taking place around her.

A few years ago, Judyth Vary Baker appeared on the JFK assassination scene and captured a significant amount of attention claiming to have had a great love affair with Lee Oswald. In fact, if you believe her story, the pair were about to be married. I didn't know what to make of this story, so I asked Dick Russell, an expert in the field whom I trust and he said he checked her out and couldn't verify her story, which grows increasingly convoluted and less believable as time goes on. Baker is supported by James Fetzer, who writes for *Veterans Today*, which has taken the place of *The Spotlight* as a fountain for CIA misdirection ops.

The mysterious Babushka Lady in Dealey Plaza.

The Spotlight leaked an Angleton memo mentioning E. Howard Hunt that began a staged confrontation between Hunt and Lane, a meaningless rabbit hole since Hunt had nothing to do with the operation, other than being placed in Dallas that day by Angleton as a potential rabbit hole. This was soon reinforced when photos of the Three Tramps were first released and mistakenly ID'd one as Hunt.

Meanwhile, *Veterans Today* claims Sandy Hook never happened and Fetzer tries to position himself near the center of the 9/11 Truth Movement. I put him in the same bag as David Icke and Alex Jones. Maybe now you are seeing how these operations really work and how real whistle-blowers will always quickly be attached to fakes in order to muddy the investigative waters? And how people looking for 15 minutes of fame and glory are played by these operations.

But these attempts by (the now-defunct) *Spotlight* and *Veterans Today* to muddy the waters, are actually a window on the cover-up, and if you follow the breadcrumbs, they'll lead you into the heart of the conspiracy.

The Real Story

The assassination was directed within the CIA through James Jesus Angleton's "Executive Action" program, which was founded by William Harvey at JM/Wave, and through the Sicilian men-of-honor society via head of the Chicago outfit, Sam "Mooney" Giancana. This might have been a result of the oligarchies running North America and Europe reaching a consensus Kennedy needed to be eliminated or it could have been a much smaller conspiracy deep inside the NSA, Pentagon and/or Sullivan and Cromwell.

After Harvey had a blow-up confrontation with RFK at the White House, the Kennedy brothers wanted Harvey sacked but Angleton transferred Harvey to run the Italian station. Soon thereafter, the ZR/Rifle was put back in action, only this time, the target was not Castro, but JFK.

The connection between Roselli and Harvey had been initiated through Howard Hughes' second-in-command Robert Maheu in discussions with Chicago Godfather Giancana. Maheu had started his career as Chicago FBI second-in-command under Guy Bannister, who also figures in the assassination. The connections between the Sicilian and Jewish organized crime families and the CIA run deeper than people realize (Giancana called them "two heads of the same coin"), although the proposed assassination of Castro was first time this alliance had surfaced since it first appeared when Lucky Luciano cut a deal with ONI during WWII. Oswald was an expendable patsy who worked undercover for the CIA and FBI.

James Jesus Angleton.

Like Giancana, Roselli made his bones under Al Capone as a triggerman. He evolved into Giancana's eyes and ears, first in L.A., then in Vegas. Once when Roselli was up on a murder charge, the witness and the investigating DA both turned up unexpectedly dead. Charles Nicoletti, one of Giancana's favorite hitman in Chicago, was also recruited. Roselli confessed his role several times, to his mistress and to Bill Bonanno while in jail. Roselli turned up dead before he could testify to Congress a second time (he'd already broken omerta by revealing the CIA-mob plot to kill Castro).

Roselli was introduced into the prestigious Friar's Club in LA by Frank Sinatra, where he discovered a fixed card game fleecing operation was ongoing and demanded a cut of the action. Soon, Roselli would be the one going off to jail for running the scam. His lawyer tried to get this case dismissed, claiming his client had done work in the interest of National Security. That defense tactic didn't seem to gather traction but it likely reveals how Angleton and his bosses (Dulles, Rockefeller) could have sold the hit around the corridors of the Eastern establishment. Possibly a "mission impossible" file was put together suggesting JFK was, in fact, a KGB agent. Also Harvey whacked Giancana, who controlled Jack Ruby. Jack may have been in charge of doing the hit on Oswald, which got botched in the field, so he was forced to step in and take care of Oswald himself. Oswald was never supposed to be taken alive. The end game reveals Angleton and Harvey arm-chaired into forced retirement, with Giancana, Roselli and Ruby all assassinated. Yes, the CIA and various crime organizations work together, but in the final analysis, it's the CIA who plays the role of big dog.

Roselli claimed to have taken the fatal head shot and was treated by anti-Castro Cubans in prison as their conquering hero, but that dishonor fell to Harrelson, the shooter on the knoll. Roselli said he was positioned in a storm drain under the overpass and his only shot went through the windshield and caught Kennedy in the neck (which would force a quick change of the windshield). Bill Harvey was positioned inside the sniper's lair of the Texas School

Book Depository, and his bullets hit Kennedy in the back, while another struck Texas Gov. Connolly. Harvey remains lead candidate as the team leader, although Dallas was flooded with shooters and spooks that day, some from the mob, others from military intel, and others from overseas. Shackley and Morales were likely on the Sixth Floor with Harvey as men looking like them were observed fleeing the scene. It's possible few on the inside realized the total extent of operations. Some mafioso believe to this day it was actually their hit, and fail to understand the complex role played by the military and intelligence networks in setting-up and covering-up the affair. According to Giancana, the shooters were paid $50,000 each, cash provided by the Texas oil crowd. As you move higher up the chain, you find George H.W. Bush of the CIA reporting to Hoover on the activities of "misguided Cubans" in Dallas that day. Bush's father helped fund the rise of Hitler and was certainly a player in the establishment after liberating Geronimo's skull from its burial site at Fort Sill and bringing it to that occult house of worship at Yale University, where, no doubt, present inductees gather around it for ceremonial photographs.

The Three Tramps

Thanks to Lee Bowers, an alert railroad employee with an unobstructed view of Dealey Plaza during the JFK assassination, three men fleeing the scene and hiding in a boxcar in the train yards were picked up and escorted to the nearest police facility, where they were apparently released without being photographed or fingerprinted. Bowers would later testify that he heard three shots, one coming from the grassy knoll and two from the mouth of the triple underpass. Bowers died a few years later, before public awareness of the three suspicious men emerged. The men are not mentioned anywhere in the Warren Commission Report, although seven pictures were taken of them by three different photographers.

Anyone with knowledge of law enforcement procedures immediately recognizes something amiss with these policemen, who seem little interested in the men they are escorting, one of whom carries a large paper sack, and all of whom must be considered suspects in just having murdered the President of the United States. Although wearing Dallas Police uniforms, no member of the Dallas Police would ever be able to identify either of them.

The Three Tramps.

The previous picture clearly shows the three faces of the "tramps." Notice the woman in the background holds her hand over her mouth. Apparently, she believes JFK's killers are being paraded before her, while one of them smiles with satisfaction.

In the late Sixties, Richard Sprague and Bernard Fensterwald formed the Committee to Investigate Assassinations (CITA). Sprague was a photographic buff who'd assembled the largest private collection of JFK photos and later became the DA of Philadelphia. One of his more bizarre theories was that a dart had been fired out of an umbrella, and that was the source of Kennedy's neck wound and real cause of death.

85

In Illinois, where I grew up, the most brilliant conspiracy researcher was Sherman Skolnick, who'd brought down a federal judge in Chicago before becoming immersed and entangled in the JFK psyops. Although his research remains impeccable, Sherman had a bit of a blind eye on Mossad elements, tending to blame most drug trafficking on the Queen of England. In reality, presidents and heads of state are largely ceremonial and not typically involved in planning or executing the complex war plans, operations that begin with the beating of a psyop drum. Study all the characters who came out of the woodwork to collect and control information on the JFK assassination, because most of them turn out to be spooks, and in hindsight Sherman appears to be one of the few that wasn't.

CITA held their conference on the anniversary of the JFK assassination in 1973, and upon arrival Skolnick began verbally attacking Fensterwald, accusing him of being a CIA stooge and holding these conferences to find out what real researchers like him were uncovering. At the time, Fensterwald was defending Watergate burglar James McCord, the suspected CIA mole inside CREEP's plumbers, and Skolnick demanded an independent panel. He got it. But when Skolnick's panel began, a kook named Amos Hickock began raving about assassination links to the KGB and also announced the Three Tramps were Hunt, Barker and Sturgis of recent Watergate fame. The links from the Kennedy assassination to Watergate were just surfacing, and this was certainly an explosive allegation that tore through the research community like a tornado!

Here's a little-known factoid: Four pictures of the Three Tramps were first published in *Computers and Automation* in an article by Richard Sprague on the same day the Watergate burglary appeared in print in the *Washington Post*.

Also attending that conference in 1973 was A.J. Weberman, who would soon team up with a former McGovern staffer to write a book called *Coup d'etat In America*. Weberman was a real character. One of the original Zippies, he was also a huge pot dealer on New York's Lower East Side, and used some profits to help fund a military training camp for potential Mossad agents in the Catskills. Weberman operated with near-impunity for decades before he got ratted out by a former associate who turned State's evidence and gave up the info on his secret Dutch bank account. After serving his time, Weberman wanted to immigrate to Israel, but couldn't take the theocracy and quickly moved back to New York, where he seems to be a dirty tricks operative for the Democratic Party these days. When asked about Mossad connections to 9/11, Weberman explodes and orders me to leave the country while accusing me of being "a self-hating Jew." Real independent research does not seem to be in the forefront of his activity list these days.

Chip Berlet is a close associate of Weberman's. And when Weberman was researching his book on the JFK assassination in Washington DC, he often stayed at Berlet's apartment. His real name, by the way, is John Foster Berlet, son of Reserve Army Lt. Col. George Numa Berlet, Jr. Berlet mostly spent the late sixties and early seventies photographing tens of thousands of demonstrators at peace and/or pot rallies, something that surely would have been a valuable resource for intel.

And suspiciously enough, Berlet was on the staff for the CIA-infested and controlled National Student Association, while his mentor, David Ifshin would go on to become general counsel for the American Israel Public Affairs Council (AIPAC). Meanwhile, Berlet evolved into the primary mainstream source for debunking conspiracy theories involving the Federal Reserve. Berlet invented the word "conspiracism," a fake disease that one day may be enough to get us all locked up on psyche wards for not believing the official stories handed down by the major media to explain events like JFK assassination or 9/11. Berlet has helped construct the future modern inquisition, where independent researchers become excommunicated agents of the devil just for holding heretical beliefs.

The upshot of Weberman's book was that two of the Three Tramps were Hunt and Sturgis. Thus the Three Tramps photos became an opening salvo of disinfo on the CIA's Watergate misdirection operations. Watergate was actually a CIA-sponsored coup against Nixon, who had little clue of the forces rallied against him, just as JFK had little clue of the CIA-sponsored trap he drove into in Dealey Plaza that day.

Weberman claims to have solved the case in 1975, and in a way, he did, for the book speculated that the head of counterintelligence of the CIA headed the assassination, and it was run through an executive action program initially set-up with mostly Cuban exiles, and the reason they killed Kennedy was because he was working towards peace instead of war. Early on, Weberman didn't mention anyone by name (except Hunt and Sturgis), which seems odd, especially since the head of counterintelligence was well-known at the time: James Angleton. However, Weberman's basic outline of the facts in 1975 was completely correct. But by insisting Hunt and Sturgis were the shooters, and that the Tramps photo proved this, Weberman, in fact, created a rabbit hole that sucked up most of the research community. It would take years for the real Tramps identity to emerge. Meanwhile, the Silvia Odio incident (which proved a conspiracy beyond Oswald) was documented in the book, but never really picked up on and run with until Anthony Summers came along many years later.

If anything, Hunt and Sturgis were used to deflect attention away from the real killers. They were fixers and experts in propaganda and disinfo. Sturgis was probably to the JFK assassination as Lt. Vreeland was to 9/11.

The identity of the Three Tramps may have been finally revealed when Chauncey Holt, a documents forger for the Lansky Syndicate, confessed as he was dying from cancer. He identified the other two in the photo as CIA agent Charles Rogers and CIA asset Charles Harrelson (father of Woody). Holt wrote *Self-Portrait of a Scoundrel*, published by Trine Day.

As to be expected, a disinfo story was soon trotted out to dismiss Holt's confession when a government researcher would locate the names of three men taken into custody that same day. These men were actually booked, however, and their names were taken. They were identified as Gus Abrams, Harold Doyle and John Gedney. Two of the men were located alive and they supposedly "confessed" to being the Three Tramps. Case closed!

Only when Houston police photo expert Lois Gibson examined photos of all the people supposedly involved, she quickly dismissed Abrams, Doyle and Gedney, while stating with absolute certainty that the Three Tramps were, in fact, Holt, Rogers and Harrelson. I cite all this just to give you an idea how deep the rabbit holes go when it comes to investigating deep political events. Whether they realize it or not, there are more writers working for the CIA's disinfo system than there are working to uncover the truth.

A Secret Order

Deep political research is a wilderness with few water holes, but many dry wells and tons of smoke and mirrors. There's far more money going into producing propaganda than real research. Just turn on your TV and watch the parade of documentaries on aliens. Or if you don't like aliens how about the secret history of

Christianity (although, curiously, none mention the cannabis-Christian connection). But just try to find something about Dimitre Dimitrov, an important whistleblower who disappeared while making overtures to President Carter to break open the JFK case, and you won't find a Wikipedia page.

A few years ago Hank Albarelli wrote a groundbreaking book on the death of Frank Olson, a chemist working on weaponizing LSD for the CIA. After spending years poking around Ft. Detrick where Olson worked, Hank turned up evidence Olson was murdered because he violated the CIA's version of omerta by telling someone about a French town they'd poisoned, resulting in four unexpected deaths and tremendous traumas.

Hank's research trailed into MK/Ultra and the Kennedy assassinations. And then came Hank's *A Secret Order: Investigating the High Strangeness and Synchronicity in the JFK Assassination (*Trine Day*)*. Unlike many researchers, Hank remains a detached observer of facts, and always keeps a keen eye for rabbit holes. The Kennedy case is filled with them, which just shows how complex the planning was for the operation.

Thanks to dozens of citizen researchers, however, the JFK case has largely unraveled in the last few years, and this book does an excellent job updating the reader on latest developments. I particularly loved the chapter on Dimitre Dimitrov, an anti-communist leader in Bulgaria, who was imprisoned after the CIA caught him trying to sell secrets to France, a dangerous game often played by spooks looking to exploit multiple sides of the fence. I have a feeling Dimitre's going to make an appearance in part two and I'm looking forward to it. Long before Guantanamo existed, Dimitre was renditioned to a torture center in Greece and worked over. He didn't talk much about those years, but did reveal they put his finger in a vise right away and kept squeezing until it turned into a bloody mess. Lots of drugs and electro shock, no doubt. When it was determined he hadn't done anything serious enough to warrant execution, he was sent to a brainwashing center in Panama and held there for years while they massaged his mind. Then they made him a CIA-connected general with a name right out of a Nabokov novel. But at some point, I guess the brainwashing wore off, the years of torture got the best of Dimitre and he decided to spill the beans.

The great thing about Hank's work is he never jumps to conclusions, just shows how activities at Langley, Ft. Detrick and other MK/Ultra locations all point to a secret order in the seeming disorder.

Of particular interest today is a description from a hypnosis expert who claimed Oswald was under hypnosis. The evidence, according to this doctor, was in how Oswald had no escape plan after his crime, yet the crime itself required complex advance planning. Instead of getting away, Oswald went home to retrieve his revolver, walked deeper into a residential neighborhood, sneaked suspiciously into a theater, and, then, when the lights were turned on and he was surrounded by officers, he drew his revolver and fired. The gun did not go off, otherwise Oswald never would have lived to say the word "patsy."

Now this doctor suspected the brainwashing had taken place in Russia, but today we know Oswald was likely worked on quite early in his life in New York, and later in New Orleans, Japan, and possibly Dallas shortly before the assassination. I find the similarities between Oswald's post-event behavior and the situation with the Boston bombers chilling. The reality is that mind control is very real and the technologies have likely progressed beyond our comprehension. I wonder if the technology is so advanced at this point they can capture subjects just via the Internet.

When I met Richard Belzer we immediately launched into a deep conversation about JFK. He was a huge buff on the subject, like me. At the time, I'd just developed a theory and I tested it out on him: "What if Angleton prepared a report for the National Security Council stating JFK was the Russian mole he'd been looking for, and that report used to divert the kill-Castro squad at JM/Wave?" Belzer's eyes got wide when I laid that scenario on him. And now, nearly 30 years later, I still haven't seen anything that conflicts with that theory.

A Perfect Nordic Beauty

After JFK became President, the mantel of power had a transforming effect, and some spiritual changes took place in him, probably aided by LSD, which was momentarily popular as a sex-enhancing sacrament among JFK's peers in seduction, the Rat Pack. Before the Merry Pranksters handed it out to the masses for free, you see, LSD was a jet set, Hollywood and Beltway fad among the elite, passed around by Tim Leary's friend Mary Meyer for one. For sure, it was more challenging than cannabis or opium, both of which JFK probably experimented with. He had back issues and frequently took shots to relieve the pain.

But suppose Angleton discovered JFK and Mary Meyer had sex on acid. That certainly would have freaked him out. JFK was assassinating and pretty soon so was Meyer, who was Angleton's wife's best friend.

JFK already had an enormous FBI file due to his affair with Inga Arvad, a Danish beauty queen who got a journalism degree from Columbia University followed by a job at the *Washington Times-Herald*. In 1941, she thought Hitler was the kindest, gentlest soul and said so in her puff pieces that promoted him while avoiding any controversial political ideas. In fact, Inga sat next to Der Fuhrer during the Olympics, and that should give you an idea of how highly Hitler prized her. The FBI launched an investigation. She was a Danish alien and they suspected she was moonlighting as a modern day Mati Hari. Soon, they discovered this married Dane was having a torrid extra-marital affair with a young ensign in Naval Intelligence, whose father was the current ambassador to England, facts that just thickened the paranoia.

Inga Arvad.

Inga and JFK were followed for weeks and knew their every conversation was being recorded and even made jokes about it. Keep in mind, during this time, naval intelligence has just contacted Meyer Lansky to seek a meeting with Lucky Luciano. Lucky is in prison but naval intelligence wants to offer a deal. If the Sicilian men-of-honor society will become spooks for naval intelligence and help root out German spooks seeking to infiltrate the docks of New York, then Lucky might be released from his 50-year sentence for prostitution.

Lucky was soon moved to a nicer prison and started getting treated a lot better. Oh, and all those strikes on the docks that had been taking place? Those mysteriously disappeared until after the war was over. One wonders what other potential deals were being tossed around in these secret meetings. One thing for sure, after

93

the war, Lucky got his "get-out-of-jail" card, was swiftly deported back to Italy, where he rapidly built the world's biggest heroin syndicate. Meyer Lansky was his financial adviser and Meyer's role included concealing American-based profits through a CIA-connected bank in the Bahamas.

When JFK's superior at naval intelligence found out about the romance, JFK was transferred to South Carolina due to his knowledge "that could be more than a bit embarrassing." Did that knowledge include the working relationship between naval intelligence and the Sicilian men-of-honor? JFK always believed Hoover was the person behind the surveillance and that sudden transfer, but he'd get his revenge by putting his little brother in charge of Hoover later in his life, which could be why Hoover willingly entered a conspiracy to eliminate JFK in this matter of national security. Between the two of them, Angleton and Hoover held enough power to control the Warren Commission investigation, as well as the post-assassination propaganda in the national media, but they could not have acted without the consent of the Eastern establishment that controls our banking and oil cartels, the real forces behind our national security services.

It cracks me up when people say they don't believe in secret societies, when, in fact, nobody discounts that a Sicilian brotherhood-of-death runs what's left of the organized labor movement. One only wonders how long it will take before similar brotherhoods emerge from high society or the Pentagon. Secret societies are everywhere and always have been. Most are just clubs and fraternities where ritual and ceremony is celebrated in secret because keeping your ceremonies private is one way to invest power in them, just ask Freemasons or Mormons. And, of course, if your ceremonies involve death and destruction, you'll want to keep them secret.

If JM/Wave hadn't assassinated JFK, where would our economy be today? Instead of wars in Vietnam, Panama, Iraq, Afghanistan, and so on, JFK might have declared war on bigotry, poverty and disease. Instead of drifting into a dark space ruled by sorcerers of death whose drones now encircle the earth, we might have had real freedom and compassion for all.

Sylvia Duran

Silvia Duran served as a receptionist at the Cuban Embassy in Mexico City at the height of the cold war, certainly a strategic position, and one she held when she supposedly met a dashing spook named Lee Oswald. She was already somewhat known in the intelligence community as the sometime mistress of the Cuban ambassador to the United Nations.

I know, you've probably been given the impression Oswald was a stumbling dweeb with an IQ around 60, but, in reality, he was a spook, one of the deep, deep agents. So deep, in fact, almost no one else in the FBI or CIA had any idea of his true relationship with his government.

One of those few was David Phillips, who ran anti-Cuban operations for the CIA from his base in Mexico City. Oswald was placed into those operations when he arrived in New Orleans after departing Russia. Phillips was most likely Oswald's case officer since some Cubans from JM/Wave later reported meetings where Phillips and Oswald were together, only Oswald sometimes used another name and Phillips was known as "Maurice Bishop."

Oswald was reportedly in Mexico City only a short time, but long enough to have a brief liaison with the attractive Duran, a possible affair that would become the obsession of Winston Scott, CIA chief in Mexico City (who apparently was not privy to the JFK assassination plot, having been purposefully kept out-of-the-loop by his old friend Angleton).

David Atlee Phillips.

Strangely, however, when Duran was finally deposed for testimony by the House Committee many years later, she was shown a photo of Oswald and replied, "That is not the Oswald I met in Mexico." In fact, two photos emerged of an Oswald in Mexico, one at the Cuban embassy and one at the Russian embassy, and those photos don't match nor do they resemble the real Oswald in any way. Since both those embassies had some of the heaviest surveillance in the western hemisphere, one wonders why no authentic photos nor voice recordings have ever emerged to conclusively prove the real Oswald was in Mexico. And, of course, Oswald denied going to Mexico, just like he denied shooting anyone.

Many years before Kim Philby was identified as the KGB mole inside MI6, Scott had voiced those same suspicions to Angleton, who brushed them aside, so their history was complex. Scott's next-in-command, Anne Goodpasture and Phillips, were closer to Angleton. Philby had enjoyed many all-night drinking sessions with Angleton, while milking secrets. Eventually, Philby bolted to Moscow just as internal affairs at MI6 was closing in, which left

Angleton looking like a fool. Unless, of course, Philby was a triple agent. It seems the Soviets were never completely sure. This world of spooks can be very complex and often up-is-down and left-is-right. But Angleton seems to have developed an issue with paranoia after Philby departed for Moscow.

Scott was convinced the key to breaking the JFK assassination case was getting to the bottom of the Duran-Oswald relationship. Exactly whose agent was she and what did Oswald reveal to her? Scott was a super spook with a great sixth sense and instinctively knew something wasn't right with this story. He suspected Duran was Oswald's secret lover, despite being a married woman. So he had the Mexican police pick her up and interrogate her, roughing her up and leaving her a bit bloodied in the process.

Winston Scott.

When Angleton discovered Scott wanted Sylvia interrogated and was personally investigating the assassination, he freaked out and tried to prevent her interrogation, but too late, as Sylvia had already been seized.

Around this time, the CIA decided to pull Scott from his longstanding post running the CIA in Mexico and bring him back to Washington, a move that could have been instigated to shut down any possible investigations into JFK assassination ties in Mexico. It became obvious certain bigwigs at CIA didn't want the assassination investigated at all, which Scott thought was pretty goddam suspicious. Just like Angleton had ignored Scott's suspicions about Philby and paid the price, now Angleton wanted to block Scott from acting on his Duran suspicions. This might have been intolerable for an investigator like Scott.

Around this time, Scott decided to resign from the CIA, preferring to stay in Mexico City and run his contacts as a sort of private intelligence agency, while offering helpful advice to global corporations wanting to invest in Mexico. And he also planned to finish his autobiography.

Suddenly, there was a big fight between Angleton and Scott, mostly concerning that proposed book and also whether any evidence involving Oswald in Mexico remained in Scott's personal safe. See, when you're in the CIA or even the military, and suddenly you announce plans to resign and release a book, well, that's when you lose all sympathy inside those agencies and become the enemy instead of continuing as a trusted friend.

Of course, Scott was soon dead from a "heart attack," and immediately afterwards, agents showed up to clear out his house of sensitive material, especially the manuscript, which was taken to Washington and instantly classified, although selective bits and pieces have been released over the years.

When Angleton's crew showed up to clean out the library, they were openly hostile, and told Scott's adopted son Michael, "your father did not die from a heart attack." That message may have been delivered to insure the son didn't launch an investigation of his own.

What possibly could have tweaked Angleton so much?

Well, maybe the fact the ZR/Rifle team from JM/Wave killed JFK, while deploying Angleton's deep agent Oswald as the patsy pointing towards Cuba? Because now it's pretty evident that Shackley, Harvey and Morales were key figures, and all three were fingered by Hunt's deathbed confession, and Morales confessed separately on his own shortly before his death.

What a web Dulles and Angleton were weaving, eh? But then these guys were trained by British intelligence, masters of the arts of covert counterintelligence and black magic.

The Odio Incident

Her name is Silvia Odio and she proved Oswald was a part of a larger conspiracy, testimony that blew the Warren Commission fairy tale to pieces, so they took it, published it, and then ignored all its implications. Decades later British journalist Anthony Summers tracked down Odio and re-interviewed her and her sister. A few years ago, notorious disinfo artist Gerald "I see nothing" Posner claimed Odio was mentally unstable.

Like all military-style operations, despite impeccable planning, things immediately go wrong the instant the first wave hits the beach, and the assassination of JFK was certainly no different. Oswald, for example, was never supposed to be taken alive, a huge blunder that made the clean-up really messy. I suspect they might have preferred Oswald shot dead in the room overlooking Dealey Plaza with the open window, the Carcarno rifle in his hands. But he had moved to the lunchroom to grab a bottle of coke out of the vending machine when the first wave of police arrived inside the building. A policeman soon saw Oswald get into a Rambler station wagon and depart the scene. But instead of fleeing downtown, where transportation was available, Oswald went home and then went a movie theater in the neighborhood, likely as part of some prearranged meeting. While in the Dallas jail, he reportedly made a phone call to a number associated with naval intelligence, but someone at the switchboard pulled the plug and his only call never went through.

Sylvia Odio.

Originally, the assassination was supposed to be blamed on Castro, and used as a pretense to invade Cuba. A lot of time and effort had gone into sheep-dipping Oswald as a pro-Castro fanatic. But he was also sheep-dipped as an anti-Castro fanatic who blamed the Bay of Pigs fiasco on JFK. The Bay of Pigs is a complex story. Dulles was fired because the invasion was botched as it depended on local support to succeed, of which there was none. Castro's meager jet force remained untouched, and the invaders had no jets, so they lost the air war instantly, ending any hope of success. It was a dumb plan and depended entirely on US military support. But JFK was furious at how transparently inept it was, and refused to send in the cavalry as expected, although he did buy back the survivors, which in hindsight may not have been the brightest idea as some soon joined hit squad against him.

In 1962, Odio was visited by three men, two of whom claimed to be members of her father's organization, the Junta Revolucionanria, a left-wing organization that was anti-capitalist but also anti-Castro. They claimed the third man with them, introduced as Leon Oswald, had volunteered to kill Castro. Over the decades it's been pretty well established that Leopoldo was the Intelligence Chief for Brigade 2506, the group massacred at the Bay of Pigs, a man really named Bernardo De Torres, who later told his daughter he was in Florida the day of the assassination and had launched his own private investigation into the incident but had to abruptly halt after discovering the truth. He showed up and volunteered as an investigator for Jim Garrison after Garrison launched the only real government investigation. Yet every promising lead De Torres unveiled to Garrison led into a dead-end. De Torres' primary aim seemed to be casting suspicion on Castro as Kennedy's real killer. Eventually Garrison became convinced De Torres was secretly working with the CIA to disrupt the investigation.

After being dismissed from Garrison's inner circle, De Torres immediately went to work for super spook Mitch Werbell as an arms dealer in Latin America, and, according to some, became a major player in the narcotics trade. Gaeton Fonzi would establish that De Torres was one of the 25-odd spooks in and around Dealey Plaza that day and was posing as a photographer during the event. Apparently, De Torres kept those photos in a safe deposit box as his own personal life insurance policy.

But no matter how you slice this story, you can't continue the fiction that Oswald was a lone nut without a single co-conspirator. And as I repeatedly sift through these facts to reveal their true essence, it stands out that the scripted evolution of Leon Oswald, from Castro killer to JFK killer, is the same evolution experienced by the ZR/Rifle team inside JM/Wave.

Masonry Might Provide a Clue

I don't practice spiritual intolerance, so I have deep respect for the masonic traditions, just as I respect the histories of all the major

101

religions that support peace, non-violence and the brotherhood of all mankind under the eye of the Great Spirit that Runs through All Things.

But if you have an understanding of the history of Freemasonry, it becomes clear the JFK and Lincoln assassinations are peppered with high-ranking members of the craft holding down strategic positions at crucial vantage points, which is not to blame masonry, just to point out the obvious.

There's a lot of angles to this story, but one thing to keep in mind is that at the time of Kennedy's murder, there was supposedly no love lost between masons and Catholics in the USA. Several Popes had issued edicts to forbid Catholics from participating in the "satanic" ceremonies of Freemasonry, probably because masons had the audacity to put a Koran and Torah on the altar alongside the Bible. After Lincoln was assassinated many books were written attempting to prove the Vatican had been behind the plot, although it's hard to say what the Pope's motivation would have been, and the first was suspiciously written by the military trial judge, who was most likely trying to worm his way out of complicity in the cover-up after most of the trial witnesses were exposed as perjurers.

People have the mistaken belief our Revolution was organized almost entirely by Freemasons? Well, there was a renegade lodge in Boston that plotted the tea party and included Paul Revere as a member, but many lodges during the Revolution were packed with Tories and stayed loyal to the Crown throughout the war, and maybe even afterwards if they were doing business with the powerful East India Company, which was undoubtedly being run by masons. Is it worth noting that the original flag to have 13 red and white alternating stripes was the flag of the East India Company? The most prominent mason in America at the time, however, was George Washington, and he led one of those

102

renegade rebel lodges and invested American masonry with tremendous sparkle and that's probably why our Capitol is so incredibly masonic. The second most prominent American mason was Benjamin Franklin, and he definitely turned out to be a British spy, and is celebrated today in England for his loyalty to the crown.

In 1826, a whistle-blower named William Morgan suddenly emerged to announce masonry was a plot by the British to manipulate the country from within, a plan that was working and had already infested the upper reaches of finance, government, law enforcement and the military. Well, Morgan was suddenly arrested on trumped-up charges and put in jail, but whoops, he mysteriously disappeared off the face of the earth while in police custody. And all the police involved are masons and so is the judge and the entire grand jury that has been called. This was just too obvious a cover-up of immense proportions. Well, the ensuing outcry over the cover-up unexpectedly reached epidemic proportions creating the first third party in America, the single-issue Anti-Masonic Party, whose goal was to elect anybody to any office but a mason, and especially police and judges. Among its leaders was John Quincy Adams, one of the more powerful Boston Brahmins.

Needless to say, Freemasonry was forced to get more secret and had to lie low after that fiasco, and it even seems possible someone might have immediately created Mormonism (which looks a lot like masonry) as a possible fallback position in case the craft had to be abandoned. And I say that because Morgan's widow married into Mormonism and was one of the founder's many wives. Regular readers may recall my theories concerning the vaporous nature of secret societies and how they can disappear effortlessly by sliding inside a new entity, like some alien life form. But that wasn't necessary because the masonic scare blew over quick, and masons were able to win the next election and wound up electing a remarkable string of masons to the highest office in the land, including Andrew Jackson, James Polk, James Buchanan, Andrew Johnson, James Garfield, William McKinley, Theodore Roosevelt, William Taft, Warren Harding, Franklin Roosevelt and, most important, a former hat salesman named Harry Truman. You see, it was very important the 33rd President be a mason, especially if he was just a lowly clerk from a Midwestern haberdashery.

But at the time of Lincoln's assassination, Secretary of War Edwin Stanton took control, although Andrew Johnson was the real president. Both Stanton and Johnson were masons, although Stanton had more degrees and influence. And is it worth noting John Brown, the terrorist leader who helped spark the Civil War, was a mason and accused by some of being involved in Morgan's murder? Perhaps even more illuminating, Brown's sponsor was heir to the North American opium cartel, and founder of Yale University's Order of Skull & Bones, which had been patterned after the Illuminati, a secret society designed as a nest inside Freemasonry. Yes, Virginia, secret societies can have even deeper secret societies embedded within.

On September 13, 1882, the National Christian Association, erected a statue in Batavia Cemetery during a ceremony witnessed by 1,000 people, including representatives from local masonic lodges. The monument reads: "Sacred to the memory of Wm. Morgan, a native of Virginia, a Capt. in the War of 1812, a respectable citizen of Batavia, and a martyr to the freedom of writing, printing and speaking the truth. He was abducted from near this spot in the year 1826, by Freemasons and murdered for revealing the secrets of their order."

I believe masonry has been in decline for decades, however, and there are other, newer, more powerful secret societies in play these days (and the Bilderbergers and Skull & Bones certainly come to mind), but the bedrock most of these societies was built on remains the ritual and ceremony of Freemasonry. Meanwhile, a Mormon mafia is growing inside the CIA and the FBI, joining the already well-established mason mafia, although you'll often find either a Bonesman or a Vatican-connected Knight of Malta leading the crew.

But in regard to the JFK assassination, the fact that both J. Edgar Hoover and Chief Justice Earl Warren were near the epicenter of masonry, and that incoming President Lyndon Johnson was also a mason and so was Guy Bannister, and so were two members of Warren's Commission: Richard Russell and Gerald Ford, all speaks to the possibility that a nest of this conspiracy resided at least in part deep inside the upper echelons of Freemasonry.

One thing I do want to point out, however: there are many sites that will try to confuse you by claiming the assassination was a masonic ritual, held at a certain time and place for astrological reasons, and will go into endless coincidences to support this claim. I checked this stuff out and found it ridiculous. The assassination was headed by Harvey, Shackley, Morales and Roselli and they were cold blooded killers who could have cared less what latitude the job took place on. There were at least two previous attempts thwarted, one in Chicago and another in Miami. The time and place are not the key to this puzzle.

However, just as an outcry emerged over the masons involved in the Morgan cover-up, there should have been an outcry concerning the masons involved in the JFK and Lincoln cover-ups. Because as far as I can tell, they were running the show.

Dorothy Kilgallen

She was a Roman Catholic, and worked for William Randolph Hearst, and rose to the top of journalism and even got onto a TV show, "What's My Line," on which she displayed her insightful and penetrating mind, although her co-stars were furious when private comments made in the dressing room began appearing in her widely circulated newspaper column.

Dorothy Kilgallen.

She mostly covered show business, but loved investigating deep politics and organized crime as well. When a doctor in Illinois was railroaded into prison for the vicious murder of his pregnant wife, Kilgallen began a crusade to get him released. She became the most famous and influential journalist in America and developed such a regal style that she could upstage a monarch's coronation with jeweled tiaras and elaborate outfits.

It was likely after a cocktail party with a British intelligence agent that she rushed out her first front-page scoop regarding the existence of UFO's: "British scientists are convinced these strange aerial objects are not optical illusions or Soviet inventions, but are flying saucers which originate on another planet," she wrote, in a front-page story. "The source of my information is a

British official of Cabinet rank who prefers to remain unidentified. 'We believe, on the basis of our inquiry thus far, that the saucers were staffed by small men—probably under four feet tall. It's frightening, but there is no denying the flying saucers come from another planet.'"

Now what are we to make of this? Obviously Kilgallen was used to plant a rabbit hole of immense proportions, one that would soon explode and reverberate across the world: the aliens have landed! The purpose of seeding such disinfo into the press using an unwitting dupe like Kilgallen is obvious and bears all the markings of a Tavistock mind control experiment to see how far the alien rabbit hole could be stretched. Sheep-dipping her as a conspiracy kook was the easiest way to undermine her investigations into deep politics. Anyone asking prying questions is easily diverted with a tale of alien space ships, or "we never walked on the moon," or those clouds in the sky?—those are chemicals and not just water vapor, or any of the rest of the paranoid rabbit holes disinfo agents like David Icke and Alex Jones keep jamming the Internet with.

But Kilgallen quickly abandoned the UFO story as she was a serious journalist and when zero proof appeared of little green men or a space ship, she moved onto other investigations. She was actually considered the nemesis of Frank Sinatra, who called her "the chinless wonder" and sometimes closed his shows by urging someone to please run her over. She broke the story of Marilyn Monroe's affair with JFK, and Marilyn was dead within a few days, although Kilgallen never swallowed the story it was an accidental drug overdose and shredded the official story in her column. She may have sensed her column played a role in killing Marilyn, because it certainly appears that way in hindsight.

Kilgallen was no saint: she was a snooty upper class type who frequently put down the lower classes and detested country music.

But she was a romantic and a dedicated seeker of the Big Story, and had spent quality time in the Oval Office with the President with her 11-year-old son, and Kennedy had treated them both graciously and with utmost respect, so when he was assassinated later and then his alleged killer assassinated, she wound her way down to Dallas and scored a private jail-house interview with Jack Ruby, a conversation held out of earshot of anyone else. You see, four years earlier, Kilgallen had broken the story of the CIA and mob working together on a hit team for Castro, so it wasn't much of a stretch to suspect that same team might have been redirected at JFK.

When she returned to New York after her Texas investigation, she told her friends she was going to blow the case wide open and began working on a book, one she probably expected to win another Pulitzer.

The reason Ruby had a conversation with Kilgallen (and no other person) was because he knew how significant she was. And he was also aware of her immense knowledge of organized crime, the CIA, and their connections with a nest of anti-Castro Cubans in Florida. He probably told her everything he knew. Kilgallen did a lot of footwork as well, tracking down key witnesses, including a witness to the Tippit shooting who was never called by the Warren Commission, who said two men, neither of whom were Oswald, fled the scene. She had a source inside the Dallas police department who provided the radio log, indicating the Chief of Police called for officers to rush to the top of the overpass. (Roselli's shots had come from that overpass, but under it, as he was lying in a storm drain.)

Kilgallen spent a year researching the story and a huge break came when she landed a copy of the 102-page interview the Warren Commission had conducted with Ruby. She began publishing excerpts just to show how ridiculously incompetent it

108

was. While Ruby pleaded with Ford and Warren to take him to Washington because he did not feel safe in Texas and was eager to talk in a safer location, they said they could not arrange that. He then tried to lead their questions deeper, but was rebuffed and the conversation misdirected elsewhere. Don't you think it odd only two Commissioners, both of them high-ranking Freemasons, were sent to Texas to interview this key witness, instead of bringing that witness to the entire Commission? And why did they ignore Ruby's pleas to get out of town, while asking the dumbest questions?

The FBI wanted to know where Kilgallen got the transcript and started a whole bunch of surveillance and harassment, although I'm sure Angleton had been closely listening to all Kilgallen's phone calls as well as reading her mail after that private jail-house conversation with Ruby. Most likely, she'd been under intense surveillance the entire year.

Kilgallen was in close communication with Lane at the time, who'd captured the center of energy on the investigation by posing as an honest researcher. Too bad Kilgallen didn't know about Lane's background in military intelligence. Even more suspicious was the sudden arrival of young Ron Pataky, the handsome ladies man who had been cruising Hollywood, stalking the rising *ingenues*. He was half her age but completely infatuated with her, and quickly became her closest confidant while pumping her endlessly for the latest breaks in the JFK case. He'd later claim the relationship was "platonic."

On November 8th, 1965, Kilgallen was discovered by her hairdresser. She was lying in bed as if she had fallen asleep reading a book, although she couldn't read without glasses, it's a book she finished days ago, and the book is turned the wrong way around. She is fully made up, even wearing false eyelashes, and also wearing some ridiculous outfit, not her usual worn out pajamas. Even more suspicious, she's not even in her own bed, but one on a lower floor, a room she seldom visited. The hairdresser knows something is amiss with this picture, and calls the in-house staff, so they can notify the police. He immediately exited through the front door, where he was stunned to find a police car with two officers parked directly in front of the house, as if waiting for a call to come in, as if they knew a dead body was already inside and wanted to be the first at the scene.

Obviously, the autopsy was a joke and cause of death listed as "indeterminate." Funny thing is, the doctor refused to sign the certificate and apparently had another doctor sign it in his name. Lane showed up quickly hoping to score the accordion file on JFK. Kilgallen's not-so-grieving husband turned him away and when questioned by anyone about the precious files, would only say "I'm afraid that will have to go to my grave with me." The hairdresser was so upset by some of the attitudes, he refused to attend the funeral. Another strange person missing from that ceremony was Pataky. In front of everyone at the funeral, Kilgallen's mom accused her daughter's husband of complicity in murder. It must have been a very dissonant ceremony.

I know Lane has been sheep-dipped as a knight in shining armor since the beginning of this saga. And he defended a famous libel case against Hunt, but I am afraid it was all most likely a staged operation because Hunt was a rabbit hole Angleton had placed in the story, and numerous ops were run to point towards Hunt and Sturgis and make them the shooters, but if you check on Lane today, you'll find him closely related to the Holocaust Denial movement, something obviously created by spooks. And that's the real value of time. After fifty years or so, the wolf spots begin appearing on those sheep-skin overcoats. And like a scene out of *The Bridge on the River Kwai,* the muddy river is descending and lines can be seen leading towards the CIA.

And as for Pataky, he picked up a master's degree from Jerry Falwell's Liberty University, and then a PhD in Christian Counseling from Trinity Theological Seminary, although a rumor did appear a few years ago that he'd dropped out of Stanford in the early 1950s to attend an assassin's training school in Panama. In 2007, Pataky was interviewed by *Midwest Today* and said he felt the odds Kilgallen died accidentally from drinking too much and taking too many sleeping pills was around 75%.

Now do you see how far these games really go and how deep the rabbit holes really are, and how easily the press can be manipulated by people in power?

Amos Eunis

On November 22, almost all attention in Dealey Plaza was fixed on the President and First Lady as they rode slowly through the plaza in Dallas at under ten miles per hour. Only four claimed to have glimpsed a gunman in a window of the Texas School Book Depository, and not all agreed which window. But because this territory is so salted with spooks and rabbit holes, you never know whom to trust, if anyone. The youngest and most believable witness, however, was a 15-year-old named Amos Eunis who led the police at the scene to start searching the School Book Depository after seeing a man fire twice from its corner window.

Amos heard four shots that day, and was certain two had been fired by a bald-headed man in the southeast corner of the 6th floor. He saw a reflection off the head when the gunman leaned forward to take his second shot. The fact he could not identify any other characteristics may have saved Amos's life for had he gotten a good look at the shooter's face, he would have known it wasn't Oswald, who was downstairs finishing his lunch. Many inconvenient witnesses died prematurely, the first wave right after the event and another when Garrison began his investigation.

When I began researching a cover story for *High Times* magazine on the assassination, the most illuminating book I discovered was *Wilderness of Mirrors* by David Martin, my first real look inside the CIA. The book revealed Bill Harvey and Johnny Roselli had been working with Ted Shackley and David Morales on a plot to assassinate Fidel Castro, a project halted by the Kennedy brothers.

My immediate suspicion upon reading the book was that Harvey's executive action project diverted to hit JFK after the President demoted Harvey, who had a purple hatred of both Kennedy brothers. When RFK suggested he could train some infiltrators on his estate, Harvey had snorted: "Train them as what? Babysitters?" Harvey, on the other hand, was the CIA's most gung-ho, boom-and-bang cowboy, an assassin with many notches already on his gun, and certainly dreamed often of killing JFK whether he acted on the impulse or not. Harvey had a serious drinking problem and issues with rage. The CIA takes orders from the National Security Council, which is chaired by the President. But what if the council decides the president is a threat to national security? Could the council then deploy the CIA to remove him? Because apparently that's what actually happened.

If it was Harvey's bald head Amos saw that day, it means Harvey flew in from Italy where he was running the Rome CIA station, a post that deployed a corporate front named Permidex to cloak covert ops. Clay Shaw, one of Oswald's CIA handlers in New Orleans, also had a connection to Permidex and CIA operations in Italy, which were some of the dirtiest imaginable and included a secret right-wing militia fomenting terror and blaming it on left-wing Communists. The activity was being directed through a Masonic lodge named Propaganda Due (P2) and membership ran deep into the Vatican, the Italian military and the secret services.

Twenty-six years ago, I called Martin while researching my JFK story. He was working at *Newsweek* or AP at the time, but would soon rise to the prestigious post of National Security Advisor for CBS News. I asked if Harvey was involved in the JFK assassination. "I never heard that," deadpanned Martin. Today, I realize he was likely not being completely truthful as rumor inside the CIA ran rampant that Harvey had been one of the shooters, along with Johnny Roselli. There had to be at least one more shooter, however, and that would be the man who took the fatal shot from behind the picket fence on the knoll. The most likely candidate is Woody Harrelson's dad, who is serving a life sentence for killing a federal judge, but he has denied involvement, although Charles Harrelson was photographed attempting to flee the scene as one of the three tramps that day.

Anniversary Books

You know the CIA brought out some big guns to create a cloud of smoke around the JFK assassination for the 50th Anniversary. Former *New York Times* reporter Philip Shenon has worked for years going over all the recently released documents. He was on *Face the Nation* and went over some of the more bizarre details of the case, dots that he just doesn't seem to be able to properly connect. The book received a massive review in the *Washington Post.*

If you've been following my analysis of this case, you understand that the murder of Win Scott is a key element because Scott did his own investigation into Oswald's trip into Mexico and wanted to shine a spotlight on his alleged relationship with a woman who worked at the Cuban Embassy, a woman he suspected may have even been a double agent for someone.

Shenon did cover some of the incredible destruction of evidence that started two weeks before the assassination when Oswald delivered a note to the Dallas FBI, a note that was quickly destroyed. The destruction continued for months afterwards. Never has so much important evidence in a murder case been so recklessly destroyed. Oswald's note may have indicated a plot against the President, or revealed his role as a deep undercover informant for CIA counterintelligence. We will never know what was in Oswald's note, just like we will never know what was written on the official autopsy, the notes of which were immediately burned. Oswald also tried to leave a note at the Dallas police after he was taken into custody, and that note was also immediately destroyed by the police.

There were tremendous machinations inside the Warren Commission to conceal and destroy evidence and limit the investigation. This critical woman from inside the Cuban embassy in Mexico was not interviewed even though she seemed to have crucial knowledge. The reason? According to Shenon, Chief Justice Earl Warren explained: "We do not interview Communists." This seems especially odd since one of his staff actually contacted Fidel Castro about the case. There was a lot of early effort to paint Castro as a possible controller of Oswald, an effort that was quickly abandoned when it was decided he would forever remain a "lone nut," which is the preferred way for intel to conduct assassination ops.

Bob Scheiffer intro'd his segment on the book by stating upfront it comes to the "right" conclusion, which is Oswald acted alone, even though the evidence of a massive cover-up is overwhelming at this point, which just goes to show how controlled the US media is. After 50 years no cracks in the official story are allowed, even though the entire disinfo facade has crumbled and even people like me are cracking the case open now that so many whistleblowers have come forward over the last 50 years.

I solved this case years ago. The ZR/Rifle team assembled to kill Castro (Harvey, Roselli) was diverted for the Kennedy hit and immediately afterwards, a trail of dead bodies began appearing around Angleton, one that included some of his friends, as well as his old buddy Win Scott, who'd become dangerous after he kept pursuing his own private investigation into the assassination.

But there's no way Angleton instigated the plot or even pulled it off without the complicity and direction of Dulles and Hoover, as well as some highly-placed people inside the Pentagon. I'd assume the cabal reached into the star chamber of the oligarchy. The Texas oil crowd (Hunt, Murchison) put up the $150,000 cash to pay the shooters, but they were just a burn layer.

We've passed the 51st anniversary of the JFK assassination and a slew of new books have been released, including some that were helped along by CIA assets to keep mud in the water. There's no scorecard and no way to tell which are real and which are limited hang-outs or outright frauds. Oswald's alleged mistress came forward, as well as the offspring of Operation 40 assets, and there's the deathbed confession of Hunt. Trine Day has an autobiography of Chauncey Holt, Meyer Lanksy's accountant, forger and occasional pilot, who managed to outlive his gangster and CIA associates, which might explain why he was able to tell his story. You might recognize Holt as one of the tramps photographed in Dallas. The other two have since been identified Charles Harrelson (Woody's dad) and Charles Rogers, although when the photos first surfaced, a huge effort was made to convince the research community that Hunt and Sturgis were among those tramps. It was Angleton who planted the story Hunt was in Dallas that day, which was true, although Hunt likely had little idea what was going down as he was a propaganda expert and not an assassin. Spooks and gangsters play their games with limited background info, usually some made-up cover story. Everything is intel rules: info strictly on a need-to-know basis, with most not-knowing much of anything, except to follow orders or face dire consequences. Organized crime and the intelligence agencies work hand-in-glove and the corruption is worse than you ever imagined.

Holt, like most of organized crime, did not like Kennedy and felt he'd betrayed the cause after they'd helped him steal an election from Nixon, something that happened mostly in Chicago. While attacking Marcello and Hoffa through the Justice Department, JFK was also trading secret messages with Giancana through a mutual mistress. It would be interesting to know what was in those messages because Giancana would soon be involved in assisting the assassination, sending some of Chicago's best hit men to Dallas, a list that likely included Roselli, Nicoletti, and Leo Moceri.

Although Holt died in 1997, long before this book was published, he did participate in a documentary on YouTube worth watching. Like many involved, Holt arrived in Dallas not knowing they were about to assassinate the President. Even among the spooks and gangsters at the scene there was confusion as to what had gone down and who's secret agent(s) had done the shooting.

Frank Sturgis and Marita Lorenz

Marita Lorenz was 19 when she first met Fidel Castro, having just arrived in Cuba from her homeland in Germany. She soon became Castro's lover and met an American named Frank Forini who was working with Castro. Forini's comrade-in-arms E. Howard Hunt wrote an espionage book detailing Forini's true life exploits as a spook using "Sturgis" as his cover name. Within a few years, Forini legally changed his name to Sturgis.

Sturgis had an interesting life, having been a Marine and served in Army intelligence, been a policeman, then become a pilot, and

he'd also run some bars and nightclubs in his hometown in
Virginia. Eventually, Sturgis became a full-time spook working
with the CIA and claimed to have helped trained Fidel and Che's
400 initial troops, but later turned against them after they went
Communistic. Pretty soon Sturgis and Lorenz were plotting how
to poison or blow-up Castro with a cigar filled with TNT.

Sturgis was involved in Operation 40, a CIA assassination squad,
and certainly knew some details of the Kennedy assassination, as
did Lorenz. However, both were played by the CIA and used as
counterintelligence tools to seed limited hang-outs and rabbit
holes. Although Sturgis was initially identified as one of the three
tramps, along with Hunt, this turned out to be an immense rabbit
hole. Decades would pass before researchers began to fathom the
truth. Hunt and Sturgis were used as backstops.

Frank Sturgis.

But after Sturgis was caught at the Watergate complex and
convicted, he sued the Committee to Re-elect President and the
case was settled out-of-court. Sturgis believed he was acting on
orders from the White House in a matter of deep national security,
looking for evidence involving the JFK assassination supposedly
held in a safe by the heads of the Democratic Party. According to
Sturgis, this evidence had been collected by Cuban spooks
investigating the case for Castro.

One of the major misdirections employed with the JFK operation had been to blame the assassination on Castro, which is why the designated patsy was sheep-dipped as a Castro supporter who'd just recently visited the Cuban embassy in Mexico. Sturgis was part of the plan leaking info pointing towards Castro, but he also became a major suspect in the case himself.

Apparently, Sturgis was in Miami that day, or at least he had two family members willing to swear to that alibi. I believe he probably was. There may have been several teams assembled for this mission, and it was very clever to blame the hit on Sturgis because his team wasn't used. I suspect both Sturgis and Hunt were floated as patsies by Angleton, who engineered the cover-up. Of course, Hunt wants to ultimately blame the hit on LBJ, which is ridiculous. Angleton was a Yale grad and very close to Dulles and the Rockefellers, and this Eastern establishment does not take orders from a corrupt Texas politician like LBJ, who had enough secrets he could easily be blackmailed or paid off in cash.

Eugene B. Dinkin

Unfortunately, there are no pictures of Eugene Dinkin, who was an unfortunate victim of being in the wrong place at the wrong time.

Dinkin was an army code operator stationed in Mertz, France, when he intercepted a message between a CIA-operative (probably Harvey) who had contacted French mafia in Marseilles to recruit their top assassin (CIA code name QJ/Win) for a plot against Kennedy. Apparently this plot already had the support of some Pentagon brass and a right-wing group in Texas (Murchinson and the Hunt brothers). Apparently, some top assassins from a number of secret societies were being recruited. Dinkin made the mistake of telling one of his superiors about this message, as well as his plans to alert the world in order to stop this attempt to kill the President.

Pretty soon, word came down that Dinkin was about to be declared mentally ill, so he went AWOL and escaped into Switzerland, where he attempted to alert the press at a United Nations function. He also sent a letter to Robert Kennedy outlining the plot. Keep in mind, this all happened just days before the assassination, and Dinkin was already telling people the exact date and place the assassination was due to happen.

Of course, Dinkin wasn't the only insider to blow a whistle before the event. Richard Case Nagell allegedly also sent a letter to J. Edgar Hoover outlining the plot. But neither Dinkin's letter to RFK nor Nagell's to Hoover have ever been found, and both were likely destroyed. Meanwhile, both Dinkin and Nagell were subjected to similar tortures.

Dinkin was soon removed to Walter Reed Army Hospital and worked on for weeks with drugs and electroshock therapy, and by the time he got out, his story has changed considerably. Instead of intercepting a coded message, now he'd predicted the assassination by reading coded messages in the *Stars and Stripes*. Dick Russell wrote the book on Nagell (*The Man Who Knew Too Much*) and also happened to get one of the few interviews with Dinkin and came away with the strong feeling Dinkin had been worked over pretty heavily. Meanwhile, I saw online that his son is trying to raise funds for the definitive book on Dinkin.

In the 1960s, electroshock therapy was being used everywhere, not just by MK/Ultra and other brainwashing programs, but also on teenagers who didn't seem to be fitting in. It was standard treatment for homosexuality, for example. There was no medical science behind electroshock and Ken Kesey was the first to expose the treatment for what it was: torture. Getting electroshock was a poor man's version of a lobotomy and often used to subdue patients who weren't falling into line. It often left victims mentally wrecked and shattered their personalities, which was useful if you were trying to change that personality, as in what may have happened to Dinkin.

The George Bush Connection

I guess you know Dealey Plaza was flooded with spooks 50 years ago. One young spook at the scene was George H.W. Bush, who was working deep cover for the CIA through his fledgling oil company Zapata, building platforms in the Gulf of Mexico, some of which were designed as resupply depots for the anti-Castro network operating out of Miami. There were a lot of CIA people in Dallas that day, although some may not have known much about what was about to go down.

The first piece of evidence to tie Bush to the assassination was a memo written by Hoover the day after the assassination that revealed "George Bush of the CIA" reported by phone on the activities of some "misguided Cubans." One wonders what the purpose of this memo was? Was Hoover tying a Bush family member into the scene to cover his own ass? I guess you know CIA Cuban exiles provided the support team that assisted JFK's CIA-mob assassination team? And it's only because of the testimony of some mob figures and Cuban exiles that we know what happened that day as no one from inside the CIA has ever spoken out, or at least spoken out and lived? But then something even more interesting turned up more recently.

Another memo was written the day of the assassination and claims private citizen George Bush called the FBI immediately after the assassination to point a finger at a student named James Parrott. Was this call really placed from Tyler, Texas, and how easy would it have been to place a call from a hotel in Dallas and route it through an office in Tyler for the sole purpose of giving Bush an alibi? Or maybe just to put mud in the water on the investigation? Right after a major operation like the JFK hit, propaganda teams will put out a bunch of fake info, sort of like chaff being dumped from a jet with a heat-seeking missile on its tail. This disinfo dump is intended to create just enough confusion after the event to allow the real tracks to be quietly disappeared.

Considering Bush's father Prescott was very close with fired CIA chief Dulles (and the Rockefellers) and Nixon was Prescott's protégé and Prescott was involved in profiteering off WWII by trading with the Nazi's, one imagines the Bush family is pretty deeply embedded into the establishment power structure. Which is why I suspect their possible involvement in the murder of JFK, Jr., something that happened just as another Bush was getting ready to take the Presidency. Do you have any idea of how easy it would have been for JFK Jr. to become President? And once President do you realize how easily JFK Jr. could have gotten to the bottom of his father's murder using the power of the presidency? And that is why a Kennedy will never be President in our lifetimes. The CIA and the Pentagon are not ready for information about the assassination to leak out to the public, not yet, not until all the principle characters are long dead and buried.

The Umbrella Man

The JFK assassination was a carefully planned operation, and the disinfo smoke screen started before Kennedy was in the ground. Most people have the impression Lane is a teller of truth on this issue, but I know better.

Lane was posted to Army Intelligence during WWII, a theater of operations controlled by Dulles, who went on to construct the CIA and run it—until Kennedy fired him. Lane rushed to Dallas to represent Oswald pro bono and soon found himself representing his widow, certainly a strategic position for any spook, and a position from which Lane dug some rabbit holes mined with time bombs.

Rush to Judgment was a confusing mess and even though Lane seemed to know immediately the CIA was behind the event, he never named any major perpetrator, instead focusing singular attention on Hunt, a propaganda expert and not an assassin. Lane's famous lawsuit against Hunt (for which he was paid around $5 million by the Liberty Lobby) proved nothing except Hunt could have been in Dallas that day. Lane could have gone after one of the central figures, like Shackley or Harvey or Morales, and climbed the ladder of power from there, but never tried.

I hope you realize Liberty Lobby is an obvious disinfo op that claims the Rothschilds run the world, a rabbit hole the radical right has been perfecting for centuries. Which isn't to say that they don't control enormous resources—obviously they do—but their influence is exaggerated to take attention off the oligarchies of North America and Europe, most of whom don't even allow Jews in their private clubs. But there's one particular rabbit hole with a time bomb I find fascinating, the umbrella man of Dealey Plaza.

After the assassination, when bands of citizen researchers began coalescing around Penn Jones' suspicions of a military intelligence operation, Richard Sprague ran a tiny fledgling computer magazine. Sprague was the first to publish photos of the three tramps, an event that occurred just as the Watergate scandal was breaking. Hunt had just been arrested and Nixon was saying Hunt's arrest might open up "the Bay of Pigs," his code for the JFK assassination. Helms angrily fired back that Watergate had "nothing to do with the Bay of Pigs."

Meanwhile, a signed memo by CIA counterintelligence chief Angleton was published by Liberty Lobby claiming Angleton was concerned how the CIA was going to explain Hunt's presence in Dallas that day. (Like Angleton wrote incriminating memos and had them leaked? Not very likely. Angleton did nothing by accident. The memo was an obvious plant to put heat on Hunt and deflect away from JM/Wave.) Suddenly, Hunt was falsely identified as one of the three tramps, and links from JFK to Watergate exploded. Sprague immediately started promoting a new concept: the umbrella man was the shooter.

You can see umbrella man in the photo taken seconds before the assassination. He stands at the entrance of the kill zone and opens his umbrella just as Kennedy arrives and pumps the umbrella to draw attention to it. He became the greatest mystery of the assassination and many researchers assumed he was signaling shooters to commence firing. A darker-skinned man (perhaps Cuban) standing with umbrella man appears to hold a walkie-talkie.

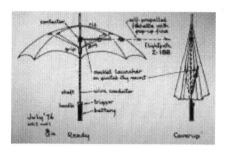

Sprague even made a diagram showing how the umbrella weapon supposedly worked. You'd be surprised how many serious researchers got pulled down into this rabbit hole. Concerns over the umbrella assassin got so intense that when Congress finally opened hearings on the assassinations, they made a public plea for umbrella man to step forward, and he did.

Turns out his name was Louie Steven Witt (three names almost seems essential for players in this drama) and he even brought the actual umbrella with him to the Capitol. He claimed he waved it as a protest symbol connecting England's appeasement of Hitler with JFK's appeasement of the Soviets. Witt was asked to open the umbrella so the Committee could be sure it didn't contain an advanced sort of weaponry.

Witt worked at the Rio Grande National Insurance Company, located one block north in the Rio Grande Life Building, 251 N. Field Street, a 19-story structure that included offices for military intelligence and the Secret Service. There's no evidence to back up his claim an umbrella was ever a symbol of English appeasement of the Nazis. In retrospect, Witt's story doesn't pass the smell test, and the diversion into the absurd umbrella-as-weapon story so easily debunked it has all the markings of a counterintelligence misdirection op to confuse people about Witt's real role.

Today, the umbrella-as-weapon story is trotted out periodically to show how absurd JFK conspiracy theories are. (By the way, Sprague, the one who invented this hoax, became attached to every serious investigation, from Garrison to the House Committee and should not to be confused with Richard A. Sprague who resigned as chief counsel for the Congressional investigation early on.)

But here's the real story: Hunt was floated as a patsy by Angleton simply because Hunt knew nothing. That's what's called "a backstop" in counterintelligence. Once Garrison uncovered the tramp photos, it should have led to the real people: Chauncey Holt, Charles Harrelson and Charles Rogers, in which case the cover-up might have unraveled quick, but instead Hunt is falsely tied in with the tramps, and then more Hunt connections are seeded to strengthened the case against him.

And that's the real problem with spooks. After they take power, you can't really control them and you certainly can't fire them because Kennedy tried that and look where it got him.

Richard Case Nagell

Here's a rare photo of Richard Case Nagell coming to court in handcuffs. Nagell was a spook with a long history of mental instability and spent decades applying for disability before he finally got it. During the Korean War he got field-promoted to captain at the record-breaking age of 20, so you know he was considered competent.

Two months before Kennedy's assassination, Nagell walked into a bank in El Paso, Texas, flourished a revolver and fired two shots into the wall. He then walked outside to his vehicle and waited for the police. When they arrived, Nagell invited them to inspect his trunk, which contained a Minolta spy camera and miniature darkroom kit, notebook with Fair Play for Cuba contacts, phone numbers of CIA officers in Los Angeles and names of KGB agents in Mexico. "I'd rather be arrested than commit murder and treason," said Nagell to the police while being handcuffed.

Nagell was sentenced to ten years for attempted bank robbery and served five for a crime he never fully explained, but later said he thought it would be a simple misdemeanor and not taken so seriously. Nagell claimed to have mailed a letter to Hoover around this time outlining the plot against Kennedy, but received no reply. Nagell made a number of claims of having evidence that never appeared.

Jim Garrison decided not to call Nagell to the witness stand during his famous trial of Clay Shaw in 1967. Garrison made the first legitimate attempt to bring forth justice but was blocked and stonewalled at every turn by the CIA. And he knew he was being led from all directions into rabbit holes salted with time bombs, and probably suspected Nagell might be one of those.

According to Nagell, after being approached by an East German spook, he was told to double down by his American handlers, so he became a triple agent, a very complex and psychologically-demanding position, but one offering a unique view on world events. While working as a pro-Marxist infiltrator in Mexico and

New Orleans, Nagell stumbled into the Kennedy plot and was allegedly told by his Communist handlers to kill Oswald to prevent the assassination (many Communists looked upon Kennedy as a potential ally). The problem with this story is there were two previous attempts planned prior to Dallas.

Dick Russell wrote the book on Nagell (*The Man Who Knew Too Much*) and it really opened a lot of doors into the assassination for me. Russell was also the first to visit Win Scott's family and get the story of Scott's feud with James Angleton over the investigation. Scott was likely killed after he tried to leave the agency after collecting evidence Oswald was a secret agent and not a lone assassin.

If you search online, you can find a bunch of Nagell's correspondence. He sometimes wrote to friends and to the media and also to Russell himself. Many of these letters are highly entertaining and show an obvious insider knowledge into the workings at the CIA headquarters in Langley.

Nagell died of a heart attack in Los Angeles on November 1st, 1995, and since he lived longer than any other whistleblower, and since nothing substantial ever emerged from any of his revelations, I think it's safe to say at this point Nagell was a rabbit hole and not a true whistle-blower. But that's how it goes in the wilderness of mirrors, where up is down, and left is right.

The CIA files

You'd think all the JFK assassination records would be public after 50 years but did you know CIA files on seven individuals are withheld for reasons of "national security?" The CIA may be withholding as many as 50,000 pages of documents related to the assassination. But it doesn't take much imagination to realize what they don't want released might help reveal what they are trying to hide, so let's look into seven mysterious people.

George Joannides was head of Psychological Warfare at JM/Wave, although he apparently lived in New Orleans much of the time, where two training camps were located north of Lake Pontchartrain. One of his primary duties was supervising the *Cuban Student Directorate* (DRE), an anti-Castro exile group. When Oswald first arrived in New Orleans, he attempted to infiltrate the DRE before starting a one-man chapter of the pro-Castro *Fair Play for Cuba*. Soon Oswald had a confrontation with some members of the DRE in the streets of New Orleans that led to newspaper and radio coverage, sheep-dipping Oswald as being pro-Castro.

George Joannides.

Immediately after the assassination, all information the press initially received about Oswald was released through DRE members in Miami on orders of Joannides. In other words, in his role as a propaganda expert, Joannides shaped initial press coverage on Oswald. Keep in mind, the assassination was essentially organized through JM/Wave's ZR/Rifle Program. So Joannides' work in this area must be viewed as psychological warfare conducted on the unsuspecting American public.

When the House Committee on Assassinations was formed in the 1970s, Congress sent two researchers to investigate the CIA files on the assassination, which could not be removed from Langley. Strangely, Joannides was brought out of retirement to stonewall and block those two investigators so all trails into JM/Wave could not be followed. But how transparent can you get, really? There should have been massive objection to Joannides as anything but a suspect in this case, and he certainly should not have been allowed to become the primary gatekeeper on CIA files..

Harvey became the CIA's go-to guy while at the CIA's Berlin station after he engineered the building of a tunnel under the Berlin Wall used to tap into Soviet communications. But after the fall of the Soviet Union, it would be revealed the Soviets had been tipped off to Harvey's operation and manipulated this listening post to leak disinfo, once again proving the KGB was often somewhat strangely one step ahead of the CIA throughout the cold war. Most of these penetrations occurred through double agents working for MI6. Strangely, the problem of double agents continued later on when Harvey's anti-Cuban operations would later to be shown to have been massively penetrated by Cuban intelligence.

William K. Harvey

Harvey instructed his wife to burn all his papers upon his death. When asked why this was done, John M. Whitten, who briefly investigated the assassination before being replaced by Angleton

129

himself, replied: "He was too young to have assassinated McKinley and Lincoln. It could have been anything." Strangely, Harvey's obvious connections to this case have yet to be explored in the mainstream media.

Morales was already the CIA's top assassin in Central America when Harvey recruited him into the ZR/Rifle project to become his number two go-to assassin after Roselli. According to Hunt's deathbed confession, Morales tried to recruit Hunt into the plot, but Hunt turned it down, which may be why he became a fallback backstop.

Phillips was one of the few CIA officials seen in the company of Oswald prior to the assassination (under the name Maurice Bishop). This sighting occurred while he was Mexico City's anti-Cuban officer, working under Scott, but not really reporting to Win in regards to Oswald. After the assassination Phillips would quickly rise to become head of the western hemisphere operations and later created the anti-conspiracy propaganda operation known as the Association of Former Intelligence Officers (AFIO), which became an important tool for holding back citizen researchers from uncovering the truth about the CIA's involvement in killing JFK.

Anne Goodpasture.

Anne Goodpasture had an interesting trajectory through the CIA. She became a special agent of Angleton's and eventually ended

130

up down in Mexico City working for Scott. Whether Scott fully trusted her, I can't say, but she was involved in hiding evidence of Oswald in Mexico and later became very close with Phillips. Although she looked like a librarian, she was a master spook and wrote a 500-page secret history of the CIA in Mexico that hopefully will one day be released.

In April 1964, Yuri Nosenko tried to defect to the USA. He was a high-ranking KGB official who had recently reviewed the files on Oswald, someone the Soviets always suspected was an American agent and not a true defector. The CIA is hiding over 2,000 pages on Nosenko and his torture under the orders of James Angleton, who sought to break down Nosenko's personality because he was contradicting Antoliy Golitsyn, a previous KGB defector who had become Angleton's pet project. Golitsyn was also favored by British intelligence, but his material was wildly unreliable. Meanwhile, the more believable Nosenko, a true defector, was treated as harshly as possible, possibly in part due to his efforts to brand Oswald an American agent. You see, Oswald was an American secret agent, and he worked directly under James Angleton, which completes this circle of info and hopefully reveals some shadows of the team that killed JFK as well as some of the major players who helped cover up that event.

Yuri Nosenko.

131

William Pitzer

You can't have a major crime without a cover-up and that operation is easy to spot when it comes to the Kennedy assassination. JFK's body was seized at gunpoint at Parkland Hospital by the Secret Service and flown to a Naval hospital in Washington for a bizarre autopsy in which the notes were immediately burned. The autopsy was conducted by two pathologists with little experience in gunshots wounds. In fact, the wounds were not even properly tracked. The entire autopsy took over three hours and seemed botched beyond belief. And then the notes from the lead pathologist were burned?

William Pitzer.

Meanwhile Jackie Kennedy and Robert F. Kennedy were located on a lower floor and couldn't understand why the autopsy was taking so long. RFK would soon call John McCone the head of the CIA and angrily asked if any of "his boys" were responsible. But since McCone had recently replaced Dulles, he'd been kept out-of-the-loop for obvious reasons. I bet RFK put an agent on determining where Harvey was that day. I've never found any evidence he was anywhere but in Italy, although I believe he flew in secretly and even tried to pick up a famous French assassin (code name QJ/Win) on the way to Dallas. Apparently a lot of the top assassins from different countries know each other by reputation. It's a private club they belong to, characters like Harvey, Roselli, Morales, Felix Rodriguez and Lucian Sarti— guys who actually pull triggers. And once you get a rep, you can work for the CIA or anyone else with money. Notice when Ian Fleming wrote about Her Majesties Secret Service, he mentioned only a handful of double "o's" and they all knew each other. Being a spook is one thing, but being a spook who kills on command is quite another.

But Commander Pitzer was a media guy and ran the film and video system used at the hospital. Apparently, the room used for the autopsy was fully wired and Pitzer secretly recorded the entire proceedings. Unfortunately, he contacted some bigwigs at some major media, probably all three major networks, and began negotiations involving this footage. Pitzer was naive enough to think he could keep those conversations secret. Meanwhile he announced his intention to resign from the Navy.

So I guess you know the autopsy was engineered to support the idea of one shooter from behind? And JFK's shot in the back could no way be tracked to exit from his throat no matter how contorted you folded his corpse? The autopsy took a long time because they had to reverse engineer the evidence, something that probably happened before the doctors entered the scene. Since William Greer was the driver and also present at the autopsy, one wonders what he really knew?

I guess you know what happened to Pitzer don't you? Yeah, he supposedly committed suicide a few days before his retirement. But around a decade ago, a special forces operative came forward and stated he'd been asked to kill Pitzer at the time, but had turned that mission down. There was no reason given, except the mission involved national security. But when you whack someone in the military, you don't hire handsome Johnny Roselli, you get a special forces assassin with a proven track record.

Of course, Pitzer was left-handed and shot in the right temple, his hands bore no nitrates and the gun was too far away to create powder burn. Nothing added up, but it was ruled a suicide anyway.

John M. Whitten

After Kennedy was killed, CIA chief Helms put John Moss Whitten in charge of the CIA's internal investigation of the assassination, which probably goes to show how little knowledge had seeped into the agency outside Miami.

John Whitten.

Whitten was doing a good job, despite being initially swamped by a blizzard of crackpot material provided by the FBI. If you want to understand why so much crazy material appears immediately after an event like JFK or 9/11, just realize it's manufactured as chaff to be tossed out of a jet shaking off a heat-seeking missile. But once Whitten spoke to Win Scott, CIA chief in Mexico, who had been conducting his own secret investigation, he realized CIA files on Oswald were being withheld by Helms and Angleton.

Whitten's investigation was narrowing down to the CIA's JM/Wave station and its key figures: Shackley, Morales, Harvey, George Joannides, Rip Robertson, Thomas Klines. Funny how just when Whitten started figuring out what happened, Helms took him off the project and arm-chaired him out of the picture. And guess who replaced Whitten? Why, James Angleton, of course. Now watch the dead bodies pile up around Angleton, starting with Win Scott.

Funny how George Joannides was brought out of retirement to act as the CIA's liason with the Congressional investigation. But you can probably understand why they keep putting the fox in charge of the hen house when it comes to this story.

You know Sam Giancana got whacked while alone with someone he trusted, making breakfast when he got a unexpected bullet in the back of his skull. According to some highly placed CIA officials, the shooter was Harvey, who would have been covering his tracks on the Kennedy killing.

After Giancana was gone, Roselli lost his power base and fled to Florida seeking refuge with the Trafficante organization. Before long, however, he wound up diced up in little pieces in a barrel in Biscayne Bay, but in his case the CIA may have just hired some Sicilian men of honor to handle that messy assignment, as I just can't imagine Harvey cutting up his good buddy Handsome Johnny like that.

H. L. Hunt

There are few characters in the JFK assassination saga that loom as large as H. L. Hunt. He was one of the richest men in the world in 1963, thanks in large part to the oil depletion allowance. I guess you know JFK wanted to end that tax break in order to reap millions for the Treasury? That alone would have been enough to put Hunt into action since Hunt controlled a vast private intelligence network, one that included the John Birch Society.

When you sift through the facts of this case, two nexus points emerge: one in Miami called JM/Wave, and the other based around the Texas oil barons who funded the John Birch Society and other right-wing hate groups, a list that included Clint Murchison and both Hunt brothers. These rich Texans were very close with right-wing elements in the military, and, in fact, had funded the political campaign of General MacArthur and supported retired General Edwin Walker, who'd been drummed out of the Army after distributing John Birch Society material to his troops. Supposedly, Oswald took a shot at Walker shortly before JFK's assassination.

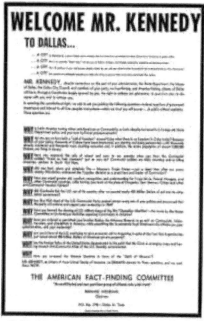

136

Hunt's son purchased a full-page ad in the Dallas newspaper the day JFK arrived. It accused the President of betraying the Constitution. In addition, a leaflet appeared all over town that accused JFK of treason. These were not random events, but obvious propaganda ploys intended to soften up the city for what was about to happen. Giancana and Nagell both claimed the Texas oil crowd put up the money to fund the assassination, and Nagell placed H. L. Hunt at the epicenter of the conspiracy. Keep in mind, Hunt was the money man behind both LBJ and Joseph McCarthy (who was actually very close to the Kennedy family). Robert Kennedy learned how to play dirty tricks from being on McCarthy's staff. McCarthy's professor of dirty tricks was a lawyer named Roy Cohn, who would soon rise to great influence.

So Hunt was a major player in the realm of secret societies. Strange, though, how the Hunts and Murchison eventually got busted down to almost nothing at one point after becoming three of the richest people in the world, which just goes to show how the real money power resides in the Eastern Establishment trusts and banks on Wall Street, and not the individual billionaires who can come and go with market trends.

Funny how the John Birch society was so peppered with Freemasons of the 33rd Degree, high-ranking officials of the Federal Reserve banking system and members of the Council on Foreign Relations. They started out attacking Communism, which they blamed on the Rockefellers and Rothschilds. But if you know anything about Communism, you know spooks set most of it up. Was there ever a time when spooks weren't running the American Communist Party? So it's only appropriate to suspect the anti-Communist movement would have been similarly set-up and run by spooks.

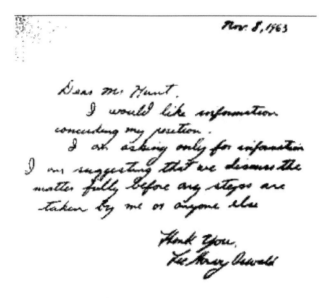

In 1975, Penn Jones received this anonymous letter, which some think was written by Lee Oswald and others claim is a forgery. This letter would soon feed right into the E. Howard Hunt rabbit hole, but, in fact, it's far more likely a note like this would have been written to H. L. Hunt, who actually lived in Dallas and is someone Oswald might have conducted secret meetings with, at least that's what Nagell claims and he seems to be one of the few trustworthy spooks in this story.

There are a couple more noteworthy points. We know one of the assassins may have been situation inside the Dal-Tex building. Jim Braden (aka Eugene Hale Brading) was one of three men taken into custody for acting suspicious in the lobby. Braden claimed to have come to the building for a meeting with Lamar Hunt, another of Hunt's sons. Since Braden had a long record and known association with Sicilian men of honor, one wonders why he was never interrogated as to what he was doing in Dallas that day? Braden would later turn up at the scene of Robert Kennedy's murder.

Another suspicious factoid is that immediately after the assassination H. L. Hunt was rushed to the airport and taken out of the country by the FBI. Supposedly, they'd received notice of a plot to kill him, an allegation later repeated by Oliver P. Revilo to the Warren Commission (although he'd declined to mention Hunt by name). But instead of protective custody, the allegedly moved Hunt to a secret destination in Mexico. Does this story make any sense except to indicate Hunt wanted to remove himself from the scene through a staged phone call? Murchison, on the other hand, held a massive victory party at his ranch, a celebration that bothered some of his domestic staff who liked Kennedy.

But then an alternative story came out more recently that claims Hunt only pretended to hide out in Mexico, and was really holed up in a five-star hotel in Washington DC, where he could more easily guide his boy LBJ in a direction favorable to the Texas oil barons. And when you talk about that Texas oil crowd and the John Birch Society, one detail to keep in mind was the name of one of the inner circle: Fred Koch. His sons now run the second largest private company in the US and created and fund the right-wing Tea Party Movement.

James Tague

Although three people were wounded in Dallas in November of 1963, you likely never heard of one of them—James Tague.

Tague was an car salesman who got stuck in traffic on Main Street in Dealey Plaza. In order to see what was causing the gridlock, he momentarily stepped out of his car expecting to see an accident blocking traffic ahead, but quickly realized it was JFK's motorcade just passing through the plaza.

Tague was standing near the triple overpass when he heard the sound of a firecracker. After another firecracker went off, something stung his cheek. Then Tague noticed people taking cover all around the plaza. The President's limo sped up and raced through the underpass. Tague was sure a shot had come from the grassy knoll. But when he walked in that direction, a policeman stopped him, and commented on the flecks of blood on his cheek and asked Tague where he'd been standing during the shooting. The policeman quickly located a section of curb that had obviously been damaged by a bullet. The blood on Tague's face was caused by a fragment of concrete kicked up by a missed shot.

Now this was pretty solid and important evidence and pretty soon that section of curb was removed for further study. However, years later, when Tague wanted to examine the curb, he noticed the bullet scar had been filled in by an unknown substance, rendering it fairly useless as evidence. Obviously, the trajectory of this bullet could have been tracked to establish the shooter's location, and if that location was anywhere but the School Book Depository, the case of Oswald as a lone assassin falls apart.

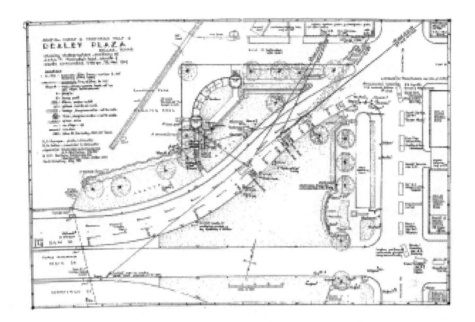

Here's an interesting map that shows where Tague was standing. In this diagram, it shows shots being fired from the School Book Depository. That may not have happened. There could have been three or four shooters. One was certainly located in a storm drain on Elm Street under the overpass. This was where Roselli says he fired the first shot, which hit JFK in the throat. Tague may not have heard all the shots, as some shooters might have deployed suppressive devices. One shooter was located behind the fence on the grassy knoll. Tague certainly heard the shots from Roselli and the knoll. This map is accurate concerning where Tague was standing, and you can see the line drawn from his spot to the Dal-Tex building. Had that section of curb been left in place and studied, the precise location of one of the shooters could have been established.

Over the years, Tague became a bit of a haunted man, like others who witnessed this crime, many of whom could not fathom why their country was covering up evidence instead of swiftly moving forward to seek justice. He wrote a couple of books, and the most recent one pointed a finger at LBJ and the Texas oil crew that put LBJ into power. Tague never really looked deeply into the CIA's JM/Wave station, or the critical role Angleton played in the cover-up.

Recently, Tague tried to attend the 50th anniversary ceremony in Dealey Plaza, but was refused admittance, obviously because he believes in a wider conspiracy beyond Oswald. How strange is it that a man wounded during the killing of a President is not even allowed to attend the official ceremony of the event 50 years later? It just goes to show what a tight lid they still keep on this story.

John Underhill

John Garrett Underhill descended from Captain John Underhill, original commander of the Massachusetts Bay Colony militia and also the primary perpetrator behind the Mystic Massacre of several hundred Pequot. His grandfather (on his mother's side) was a former general who'd played a leading role in creating the National Rifle Association.

Underhill studied linguistics at Harvard and graduated in 1937. With his blue blood, he was a natural fit into military intel and quickly rose to chief editor of the War Department's Military Intelligence Division. Following the war, he became the military correspondent for *Life* magazine, no doubt working hand-in-glove with the newly-formed CIA, staffed mostly with his wartime buddies from G2 and OSS. He acquired one of the world's largest collections of Soviet small arms outside Russia.

Beginning in 1949, he became an informant for the CIA. Two years later, he co-wrote a 6,500-word essay, "The Tragedy of the

US Army," for *Look* magazine, published February 13, 1951. According to the Harvard Alumni Bulletin, he was "recalled to brown suit service after finishing a 6,500 word article."

He served as Deputy Director for the Civil Defense of Washington, D.C., and worked on setting up "Operation Alert" in 1955, although days before it was held he claimed the exercise was "so inadequate it couldn't cope with a brushfire threatening a doghouse in a backyard," comments that led to his dismissal from the alert moments before it began.

Immediately following JFK's assassination, Underhill drove to Charlene Fitzsimmon's house on Long Island in a state of panic, and conveyed a sudden overwhelming desire to leave the country and disappear. He claimed Kennedy had been killed by the CIA's executive action team, and some people who were profiteering off drugs from the Far East. He knew the people involved, and he knew they knew he knew, which is why he feared for his own life. "Oswald is a patsy," he said. "They set him up. The bastards have done something outrageous. They've killed the President! I've been listening and hearing things. I couldn't have believed they'd get away with it, but they did!"

In 1966, when Garrison began his investigation of the crime, he'd heard about a CIA informant with important information, a detail noted in Garrison's lengthy interview in *Playboy* magazine. Garrison was eager to get a deposition from this person of interest, but before he could locate Underhill, his corpse was discovered in bed, a bullet hole behind the left ear.

A memo from the CIA to the Justice Department later uncovered through FOIA noted that Underhill had a connection to Harold Isaacs, who knew Oswald's cousin Marilyn Murret. The memo also stated Underhill was not an employee of the CIA, had

143

"infrequent contact with the New York office" and "committed suicide on May 8, 1964."

Dave Powers & Tip O'Neil

Those seeking an understanding of the JFK assassination should take note of the framing of Steven Avery, because the Avery case provides a more modern illustration on why false convictions are so often manufactured. It's not that everyone involved is part of a knowing conspiracy, just that law enforcement runs a straight line once an initial trajectory has been charted. Almost all scientific research papers are tainted by some agenda, which is why so much of today's science is unreliable. Same thing as science deployed by law enforcement.

The Warren Commission cherry-picked eyewitness testimony to JFK's murder, and even then, were forced to put tremendous pressure on witnesses to change their stories. It's well-known FBI agents instructed the witnesses: "If you didn't see Lee Harvey Oswald alone in the Sixth Floor with a rifle, it's best you didn't see anything at all." Get in line or shut up. And suddenly a few of those who wouldn't shut up, wound up mysteriously dead.

David F. Powers was JFK's personal aide and the man who spent the most time with the President outside his own family. He was riding in the car behind Kennedy's when they drove into the ambush and he never did shut up. Powers was standing up shooting 8 mm film in the backseat as the caravan departed Love Field.

On the way into town, the caravan passed a family holding a sign that begged JFK to stop and shake hands. The plea was so effective Kennedy ordered his driver to pull over. If you watch the film closely, you'll notice that whenever the limo slows or stops,

144

Secret Service agents immediately position themselves to shield the President from potential harm. Normally, the two primary agents for this duty ride a running board on the back of JFK's limo, where twin handholds were installed. Strangely, the pair were called off their usual station and moved to running boards on the trailing vehicle, the one Powers was seated in. But whenever JFK's limo slows, the two agents immediately jump off and run alongside. Unfortunately, Powers film ran out just before the caravan turned left on Elm Street, or he would have obtained the definitive recording of the assassination.

"I was assigned to ride in the Secret Service automobile which proceeded immediately behind the President's car in the motorcade," Powers told the Warren Commission. "I sat in the jump seat on the right side of the car and Kenneth O'Donnell sat in the jump seat on the left side of the car.

"At that time we were traveling very slowly, no more than 12 miles an hour…Shortly thereafter the first shot went off and it sounded to me as if it were a firecracker. I noticed then that the President moved quite far to his left after the shot from the extreme right hand side where he had been sitting. There was a second shot and Governor Connally disappeared from sight and then there was a third shot which took off the top of the President's head and had the sickening sound of a grapefruit splattering against the side of a wall. The total time between the first and third shots was about 5 or 6 seconds. My first impression was that the shots came from the right and overhead, but I also had a fleeting impression that the noise appeared to come from the front in the area of the triple overpass. This may have resulted from my feeling, when I looked forward toward the overpass, that we might have ridden into an ambush."

Powers delivered this testimony despite intense pressure to reverse and say the shots came from behind. Had these three bullets been whistling over his head, as suggested by the Warren Commission, he would have more likely felt he was riding away from an ambush than into one. Although O'Donnell had the same impression of shots from behind the stockade fence, he completely caved to the pressure and reversed his testimony to satisfy the official story. Both men were experienced veterans familiar with sounds of lethal firearms in action. Tip O'Neill, who retired after serving five consecutive sessions as Speaker of the House, wrote in his 1987 autobiography, *Man of the House*: "I was never one of the people who had doubts or suspicions about the Warren Commission's report on the president's death, but five years after Jack died, I was having dinner with Kenny O'Donnell and a few other people at Jimmy's Harborside Restaurant in Boston, and we got to talking about the assassination. I was surprised to hear O'Donnell say that he was sure he had heard two shots that came from behind the fence.

"That's not what you told the Warren Commission," I said.

"You're right," he replied. "I told the FBI what I had heard, but they said it couldn't have happened that way and that I must have been imagining things. So I testified the way they wanted me to."

"I can't believe it," I said. "I wouldn't have done that in a million years. I would have told the truth."

Dave Powers was with us at dinner that night, and his recollection of the shots was the same as O'Donnell's. Kenny O'Donnell is no longer alive, but during the writing of this book I checked with Dave Powers. As they say in the news business, he stands by his story. And so there will always be some skepticism in my mind about the cause of Jack's death. I used to think that the only people who doubted the conclusions of the Warren Commission were crackpots. Now, however, I'm not so sure."

So you have two of the nearest witnesses to the scene, located 20 feet behind the President, and both were convinced shots came from behind the fence, and possibly one from inside the triple overpass. And one of the most connected and powerful people in Congress believed they were telling the truth, which means O'Neill also believed the Warren Commissioned tampered with the evidence and made the wrong conclusions for some unknown reason.

The Nix Film

Everyone knows the story of the Zapruder film and have viewed it numerous times, on TV, in popular films, and on the internet. Yet few outside the research community are aware of an even more important film shot across the street at the same time, one that showed the picket fence on top the grassy knoll during the ambush.

The key to solving this crime is distinguishing important evidence from the avalanche of fake whistleblowers seeding rabbit holes salted with time bombs. The Nix film remains one of the most overlooked pieces of evidence, mostly because significant parts were removed, and the original fragments disappeared. We know the Zapruder film was likely worked over as well, but there was something in the footage Orville Nix shot that day that made it necessary to lower the veils completely with a magic disappearing wand.

Like many in Dealey Plaza that afternoon, Nix was convinced a shot came from behind the picket fence. After the shots rang out, most people in the plaza hit the ground. But when the shooting was over and the limo long gone, everyone raced toward the triple underpass, which was the only way to get behind that fence. All this was captured by Nix. After the assassination, the FBI visited

147

film labs and requested assistance locating evidence. They seized the original from Nix, and when he got it back, it had been cut into several segments and crucial frames appeared to have been removed or destroyed in the process.

Strangely, Nix played poker with the head of the local Secret Service and had been told by him that the Texas School Book Depository was the best spot for filming the motorcade. One would have thought the media might have interest in that detail, but Nix never got any attention beyond the first wave, and refused to talk about the assassination in later years, yet always remained convinced there was a second gunman behind the picket fence. The disappearance of the original film while in government hands is evidence of a cover-up, and it seems possible an original Nix film could eventually have been used to prove the Zapruder film was tampered with as well.

Five Shots

Eleven-year-old Mack White visited Dealey Plaza the day after JFK's assassination with his father, a local newspaper editor who came equipped with a camera. When they arrived, Mack noticed two men standing on the Dal-Tex Building fire escape, one of whom was looking through a scoped rifle mounted on a tripod.

"Look," Mack said to his father while pointing.

"I guess they're detectives," said his father. "They're probably checking to see if there was another shooter."

The idea of another shooter had not yet occurred to Mack. Later, he learned the two men could have been journalists using the gun as a prop for a photo of Elm Street that appeared the following week in the *Saturday Evening Post*. Or maybe they were something else entirely.

"In the years that followed, evidence emerged that there was likely a shooter in the Dal-Tex Building, as well as evidence for shooters all over the plaza, including the Grassy Knoll," Mack wrote much later. Like many Americans, he remains haunted by the case.

The total number of shots is a great mystery, but it can be solved. The locations of the shooters can be established at this point. Johnny Roselli was positioned in a storm drain inside the triple underpass. Certainly the first wound, to JFK's throat, came from him.

There was a man with a rifle seen in the corner of the sixth floor window, but we know that man wasn't Oswald, who was still eating lunch downstairs during the turkey shoot. There might be a shooter somewhere in the Dal-Tex Building, either on the roof or the fire escape, or deep inside some west-facing window behind a blind. A bullet from the rear hit JFK in the back, and another hit Connolly, and at least one rear shot missed everything and hit the curb, wounding Tague. This means rear shots were fired a minimum of three times, while the other two shooters seem to have only fired once. We know the kill shot came from the knoll, and it seems to have been the last, and adds up to a minimum of five shots. We just don't know if all three rear shots came from the sniper's nest on the sixth floor of the Texas Book Depository. Because two rifles were two discovered inside the depository (a Carcano and a Mauser), it's possible both might have been fired, one from the sniper's nest, and the other from the window farthest east or perhaps the roof, as both of those positions would have offered better locations from which to fire into the plaza. My best guess is there were three snipers, and the one in the sniper's nest got off three shots, while the other two fired once.

149

According to Powers, the first two shots came close together, followed by a several-second pause, and the unmistakable headshot that sounded like a watermelon exploding. Powers described a bang, bang.....bang pattern, while other witnesses heard the opposite: a bang.....bang, bang, with the last two coming very close together. Murders leave immense telepathic disturbances in their wake. Although Jackie Kennedy reacted instinctively by moving to retrieve JFK's skull fragment from the trunk where it landed, she had no memory of doing so when testifying before the Warren Commission. Yet there are multiple photos and films showing her reaching across the trunk. This is why the testimony of those nearest the scene is often somewhat unreliable.

There had to have been five distinct shots that day, but some might have overlapped and one may have emanated from a weapon with a sound-suppressor. Most witnesses heard three shots, which meant at least one must overlapped or been mistaken for a fire-cracker or motorcycle back-fire instead of a rifle shot. The difficulty is the pattern of the shots seems to vary depending on the witness's location in the Plaza.

In 1977, a cartridge was discovered by an air conditioning mechanic on the roof of the Dal-Tex building with crimped edges suggesting it had been hand-loaded or used in conjunction with a sabot, something deployed to fire lower-caliber bullets from a higher-caliber weapon. Strangely, one of the Carcano shell casing found on the sixth floor had a crimp according to Roger Craig, the first policeman on the scene. The last Federal investigation (HSCA) determined in 1978 that four shots were fired, one that missed, one at Zapruder frame 224, one at Zapruder frame 313, immediately followed by the 4th shot. The Warren Report's published FBI analysis of the bullet that wounded eyewitness James Tague indicated it originated from a weapon that did not fire full-metal jacket ammo; unlike the Carcano carbine found in the TSBD that only fired full-metal jacket bullets. This alone should have been enough evidence to prove a conspiracy.

In 1987, John Rademacher found a shell casing buried underground near the picket fence in Dealey Plaza. Through a complex set of circumstances, this shell would soon be linked to a jailed and convicted assassin connected to the Chicago outfit named James Files, who claimed he was the grassy knoll gunman and had left his shell on the picket fence. Files also indicated he had a habit of biting his spent bullets (because he liked the taste of gun powder). And wouldn't know you it, teeth marks were quickly found on the Rademacher cartridge.

Since there is such an intense effort to plant false evidence and false confessions into this story, it's unlikely in my opinion Files is telling the truth, even though major parts of his story do correspond to something close to the truth. It's far more likely the grassy knoll assassin fired once and never ejected the spent cartridge, much less put it between his teeth before setting it on top of the fence for all to see. The only shells left at the scene were the three intentionally planted on the sixth floor to incriminate Oswald. The main purpose of all these multiple fake confessions through the decades seems to be to engineer fakers into achieving widespread acceptance inside the research

151

community before exposing them as frauds. Not only do these confessions put a cloud of mud in the investigative waters, they help brand the research community as conspiracy crackpots. I call these ops: "Time bombs salted in a rabbit hole."

The one thing you notice about all these stories coming out is they almost always point the finger at LBJ, or at the Chicago outfit, or at Castro, or at the anti-Castro Cubans. This suspiciously ignores the involvement of JM/Wave (the CIA's largest station outside Langley), and most notably of Ted Shackley, David Morales and Bill Harvey, otherwise known as ZR/Rifle, the "executive action team" originally organized to kill Castro, but then diverted to kill the president in the interest of "national security."

It's fascinating to examine the details of the operation, but also important to keep in mind intel will always control the details because they are the only ones with the true facts. So don't get hung-up on minor details. It doesn't matter who the shooters were or where they were positioned or what weapons they used. It's enough to know it was a CIA-sponsored event, and the most important details are ones leading into JM/Wave. I have a strong suspicion that some secret National Security Council meetings without the Kennedy brothers may have been held in advance to fully sanction the murder at the highest possible levels.

Kerry Thornley

Intel manufactures "influencers" on both sides of any wedge issue simply because people are easily influenced. Wedge issues are the fulcrums deployed to divide and conquer. The influencer makes sure his side of the wedge flows into a managed dialectic. These games are always presented as a choice between two alternatives. If you're looking for proof of intel penetration into the emerging sixties counterculture, and the manufacture of influencers, look no further than Kerry Thornley.

Kerry Wendell Thornley.

Thornley became a major New Age influencer despite a strict Mormon upbringing. In 1963, he invented Discordianism, which became the primary influence on the Church of the SubGenius and other counterculture alternative religions.

In 1959, however, Thornley was stationed at a U-2 base in Japan along with Lee Harvey Oswald. The base was a notorious site for MK/Ultra experiments deemed too controversial for US soil and it seems Oswald and Thornley could have gone through some behavior modifications as their lives became forever entwined. When Oswald departed to Russia posing as a defector offering up the U-2 secret, Thornley moved to New Orleans and began writing a novel based on Oswald titled *The Idle Warriors.*

Thornley was subpoenaed by the Warren Commission and a copy of his unpublished manuscript entered into the National Archives. He gave a highly detailed deposition establishing what a devoted Marxist Oswald was. It included the following exchange:

THORNLEY: [Oswald] had gotten me to read *1984* and this was one of his favorites.

JENNER. Tell me what *1984* was.

THORNLEY. This was a book about…it is a projection into the future, supposed to take place in 1984 in England under a complete police state. It is, I would say, an anti-utopian novel, by George Orwell, a criticism of English socialism and what it might lead to, based upon Orwell's experiences with Communism and Nazism, his observations about a society .in which a mythical leader called Big Brother dominates everybody's life. Where there are television cameras on every individual at all times watching his every act, where sex is practically outlawed, where the world is perpetually at war, three big police states constantly at war with one another, and where thought police keep every, all of the citizens in line. Oswald would often compare the Marine Corps with the system of government outlined in *1984*.

JENNER. By way of protest against the Marine Corps?

THORNLEY. Yes; humorously, satirically. One day we were unloading, moving a radarscope off the truck and it slipped, and he said, "Be careful with Big Brother's equipment."

Because of Thornley's appearance in front of the Warren Commission, New Orleans District Attorney Jim Garrison made Thornley a target of his investigation. From Garrison's *On the Trail of the Assassins*:

Thornley had told me that he returned from his summer in California by way of Mexico City. This happened to be very close to the time that the Warren Commission said Oswald was in Mexico. By November 1963, according to his own account, Thornley was living in a New Orleans apartment he rented from John Spencer. We located Spencer, who turned out to be a friend of Clay Shaw's. As he described it, sometimes Spencer visited Shaw, the director of the International Trade Mart, and sometimes it was vice versa.

154

Several days after the assassination. Spencer told us, he came to his house and found Thornley gone. In Spencer's mailbox was a note from Thornley saying, "I must leave. I am going to the Washington, D.C. area, probably Alexandria, Virginia. I will send you my address so that you can forward my mail." *Spencer said it was quite unexpected because Thornley had at least a week left in the month before his rent was due. He went to Thornley's apartment, number "C", and found that paper had been left over the entire floor, torn up into small pieces like confetti. Before being torn up, the paper had been watered down so that the ink was blurred, making it unreadable. After the assassination Thornley told Spencer he was going to be a rich man because of the coincidence of Oswald having been the subject of his book.*

Thornley had wound up at Arlington, a Washington suburb, and had moved into Shirlington House, a first-class apartment building where he worked as doorman. Thornley stayed at Shirlington House for six months, until he testified before the Warren Commission. Oddly enough, his salary was less than the rent of his Shirlington House apartment.

In the mid-1970s when I was in the private practice of law, Thornley sent a lengthy, almost biographical, 50-page affidavit to me describing, among other things, evidence he had encountered in New Orleans of "Nazi activity" in connection with President Kennedy's murder. It was apparent that even though I no longer was D.A. Thornley wanted to assure me that he had not been involved in Kennedy's assassination. Although it did not accord with reality, as I recalled it, the affidavit had, in retrospect, one interesting feature. Purely gratuitously, it mentioned how Thornley had left Washington following his Warren Commission testimony and ultimately returned to California, where he and John Roselli happened to become friends.

Actually, the first place Thornley visited after departing Washington was Robert LeFevre's John-Birch-connected Freedom School in Colorado, where he joined soon-to-be very powerful Charles Koch. Eventually Thornley came clean on the JFK assassination and confessed he'd been drawn into the plot by E. Howard Hunt.

But we know now that Hunt was not the instigator or anything close. After David Morales offered him a role in the assassination, which Hunt turned down (according to his deathbed confession), James Angleton seems to have selected Hunt as the official agency rabbit-hole-backstop. First, Weberman falsely ID's Hunt as one of the three tramps. Then Angleton leaks a memo implicating Hunt as being in Dallas that day. Meanwhile, a handwritten note from Oswald to a Mr. Hunt is sent anonymously to Penn Jones, a leading researcher in the field before Lane shoves him off the national stage. Soon, Lane will focus all his attention on Hunt, culminating in a widely-covered libel trial. But all this million-dollar trial proved was that Hunt could have been in Dallas that day. And by shepherding all eyes on Hunt, the real culprits at JM/Wave (Shackley, Harvey, Morales) were able to waltz free.

But the Thornley saga didn't end there, not even close. In 1975, Antony Sutton published *National Suicide* detailing massive covert assistance from Wall Street to Russia. He was kicked out of the prestigious Hoover Institute and cast academically adrift. The John Birch Society seized on Sutton's work to prove a thesis that Rockefeller and Rothschild were secret Communists working to integrate Russia and the US into one entity to rule the world. Interestingly, the leading polemicist for the Birchers, Revilo P. Oliver, was also called upon by the Warren Commission for a lengthy deposition, as was Mark Lane. It appears significant depositions might have been staged by CIA-connected spooks seeding rabbit holes and backstops.

156

While working as letters editor of *Playboy*, conspiracy researcher Robert Anton Wilson was inundated by Birch propaganda and decided to counter it by writing a satirical story about the Illuminati as if the society was an honest attempt to overthrow royalty and religion (and not some covert Jesuit plot to infect Freemasonry from within). Thornley immediately began corresponding with Wilson and worked his way into the pages of *Playboy* and eventually Discordianism became the foundation for Wilson's trilogy, which began with a counterculture reporter's investigation into the JFK assassination. Wilson's fantasy, however well intended, served to make any Illuminati conspiracy less believable. Worse, it elevated Thornley to icon status instead of unmasking him as either a spook or MK/Ultra robot. Wilson's book became launching pad for decades of nutty Illuminati conspiracies.

Meanwhile, despite the loss of academic credentials, Sutton soon published *America's Secret Establishment,* revealing Yale University's Order of Skull & Bones was deploying remarkably similar rituals as the original Illuminati. He never claimed a continuous order, only that the Boner playbook had lifted significant concepts from Adam Weishaupt. Meanwhile, the Birchers kept pumping disinfo memes alleging the Rothschilds and Rockefellers were secret Communist agents plotting the integration of the US and Russia into one massive socialist state, the beginnings of the one-world government conspiracy rabbit hole.

After feeding immense amounts of disinfo to Wilson, Thornley eventually accused Wilson of being his MK/Ultra programmer. According to Thornley's latest revelations, Wilson and fellow conspiracy researcher Paul Krassner (founder of the trailblazing *Realist*), were the secret leaders of the Illuminati, a story that ran wild through the spook-infested fake conspiracy network during the early days of the Internet.

157

Meanwhile, links between the Bush family, the Boners, and the assassination of JFK would soon unravel, although most of the details were ignored by the national media. Perhaps someday the mainstream media will stop ridiculing the concept of a star chamber manipulating world events and begin addressing the evidence. This trail starts with an understanding that the CIA killed Kennedy.

Joseph Milteer

On the morning of November 9th, 1963, two weeks before JFK was assassinated, right-wing extremist Joseph Milteer was in a Miami hotel room talking with Willie Somerset, an undercover police informant who happened to be wearing a wire. This conversation was turned over to the FBI immediately, although it would not surface publicly until four years later. Here is what Milteer had to say:

Joseph Milteer.

[Killing Kennedy] "was in the working" and would be accomplished "from an office building with a high-powered rifle"....that could be "disassembled" to get it into the building and they will "pick someone up within hours if anything like that happened just to throw the public off." Milteer also mentioned "the Cubans" were involved.

Did you know JFK visited Miami within a few days of this conversation, and word of this potential assassination was well-known to the local police who enacted extra precautions to protect the President when he arrived on November 18? Probably the conspirators intended to kill JFK in Miami since the assassination was being run through the CIA's JM/Wave station there. But zero precautions were taken to protect the President a few days later in Dallas? This seems extremely suspicious given the precise details provided by Milteer. Maybe you know Frank Sturgis was accused by Marita Lorenz of driving a car with high-powered rifles and scopes in the trunk from Miami to Dallas right before the assassination? Apparently they returned to Miami by plane the day before the assassination after delivering the weapons used to kill Kennedy. Immediately before and after the assassination, Milteer was contacted by the FBI and afterwards openly celebrated the President's death. He later told Somerset: "I guess you thought I was kidding when I said Kennedy would be killed from an office building with a high-powered rifle."

Don Adams was the rookie FBI agent sent to interview Milteer before and after the assassination although he was severely limited by his bosses to asking only five questions, which struck Adams as extremely odd given the situation. In fact, the FBI seemed more interested in sweeping this incident under a rug than exploring how Milteer got his information. Adams was supposed to determine where Milteer was during the assassination, but could not conclusively establish his whereabouts during that week. Adams would eventually write a book about his investigation, one that was severely critical of the Warren Commission.

159

Here's a photo of someone who looks like Milteer standing along the parade route in Dealey Plaza, as if he'd come to watch the assassination. That fluffy hairstyle seems unmistakeable doesn't it? If so, I'd imagine Milteer attended some sort of celebration later that day. Clint Murchison held a big one on his ranch, but I'm sure there were others as many on the right hated JFK with a purple passion.

Milteer at the assassination scene.

But if you delve into Milteer's connections, you can uncover how he came to his inside information because he was the leading right-wing organizer in Georgia and helped establish both the National States Rights Party and the Constitution Party there. Among his cohorts was General Pedro del Valle, the first Puerto Rican to rise to the top of the US military, and someone later put in charge of ITT in Latin America. Del Valle fought in the Banana Wars that made South and Central America more exploitable to Wall Street bankers.

If you've been paying attention to my posts over the last month, you realize the John Birch Society played an important role in Kennedy's assassination. H.L. Hunt was a major source of funding for that organization. And if you delve into the Birchers, you find a mix of rich industrialists and high-ranking military. When the Pentagon was created right before WWII, they already

160

knew a world war was coming and the economic power in America shifted almost immediately to this newly-formed military-industrial complex, the very alliance President Eisenhower warned us against while departing office. After WWII, the CIA, our American Gestapo, was created and became the covert military force responsible for assassinating heads of state around the world if they believed too much in democracy and were soft on Communism.

Did you know Henry Kissinger believed the Joint Chiefs were a bunch of dummies easily be manipulated through propaganda? One mystery for me is trying to figure who on the right-wing knew Communism was a scam from day one, a complex set of dogmas used to mind control a generation so they could be more easily pitted against other dialectically-driven oppositional forces like Fascism and Christianity? Russia was a burnt-out rusted shell with no spare parts after WWII, and not in a position to threaten the US in any way. But they were transformed into this sinister boogie-man through propaganda.

Milteer was obviously a true believer who sincerely believed the Birch propaganda, which claimed Communism was set-up by the Rockefellers and Rothschilds to turn the world socialistic. But the name of this game has never been to create a unified one-world anything, but to milk conflict for profit. Since WWII we have existed on a perpetual war economy. To create conflict you need opposing sides. But both Fascism and the Communism were being directed by spooks to inflame conflict. It never mattered which side you joined, as long as you stayed within the boundaries of the managed dialectic.

James Jesus Angleton

In the 1960s, he was known around Langley by his CIA code name: Kingfisher.

161

James Jesus Angleton.

It's probably not a good idea to take on an exalted title like that unless you have some real power to wield and as the director of counterintelligence, Angleton was responsible for a lot of the dirty tricks at CIA during his reign. He's become the subject of dozens of books and movies, most recently *The Good Shepard,* although his multiple connections to the JFK hit never seem to surface in the mainstream media.

Angleton got his powerful post after serving as the Vatican's CIA liaison during WWII, working closely with Dulles to shield important Nazis who were given new jobs working for US interests after the war. According to Angleton, before getting his promotion, he had to promise Dulles never to put him or any of his Wall Street-connected cronies on lie detectors in order to question them about financial relations with Germany during the war. You see, many US corporations employed neutral countries to trade with the enemy, including Standard Oil, a company owned by Dulles' cousin by marriage, David Rockefeller. If you want to get really rich during war, sell to both sides.

Not only did Angleton remain in charge of the important CIA-Vatican connection, he also became the strategic CIA link to Israel and their efficient Mossad, an intelligence agency not hampered by red tape.

The sad reality is that after he got his post, Angleton was swiftly compromised by British double agent Kim Philby, who gleaned many secrets before departing back to England. Philby had spent many nights plying the chain-smoking Angleton with liquor so they could talk shop. The main subject of conversation was the suspected mole inside British intelligence who kept the KGB one step ahead of Angleton, and who might that mole be? Before long, a nest of Soviet spies (the Cambridge 5) was uncovered and a few revealed, although Philby was exonerated and Victor Rothschild never seriously investigated. Philby began working as a journalist covering the Middle East, while secretly reporting to MI6. But in 1961, Anatoliy Golitsyn, a KGB major, defected to the West and established his bona fides by offering up Philby as KGB and part of the Cambridge ring that had been operating since before WWII.

CIA spook William Buckley would write the first major book on how Angleton went crazy after Philby was unmasked. Buckley is Skull & Bones and card carrying member of the oligarchy, just like Angleton, only maybe a little higher on the pecking order. But Golitsyn was a fake defector seeding disinfo. His major thrust was that many highly placed people in Western power were really KGB, just like Philby. Golitsyn even claimed British Prime Minister Harold Wilson was a KGB spy. And he also claimed there was another KGB spy was very high up in the US government as well. Obviously, these rabbit holes served mostly to amp up Angleton's paranoia. He'd spend the next few years hunting for an imaginary highly placed mole in Washington DC, and at one point accused just about everyone in power. Did Golitsuyn also finger JFK as well as Wilson? I think this seems pretty likely. Strangely, Golitsyn became an Honorary Commander of the British Empire. And what do you think would have happened if Angleton had written a report saying JFK was a Soviet spy? Would that have justified a national security project to remove JFK from power?

But after JFK was assassinated, along came a real Soviet defector name Yuri Nosenko, who arrived in 1964. Since Nosenko did not concur with much of anything Golitsyn had been saying, and, in fact, was more highly situated and knew more than Golitsyn, Nosenko was held prisoner for four years and tortured continuously and fed LSD and other drugs in an attempt to break him down. And the entire time Angleton kept telling everyone Nosenko was a fake whose only mission was to discredit Golitsyn.

In retrospect Angleton seems borderline incompetent since he'd been played by Philby and Golitsyn. One wonders how Angleton kept his job so long, although keep in mind his files were probably more explosive than J. Edgar Hoover's.

And then, of course, there's Angleton's vast connections to the JFK assassination cover-up. It's no accident Angleton was named CIA liason with the Warren Commission and swiftly replaced John Whitten as official CIA investigator of the incident. Moves like that are made when a fox is needed to watch the hen house.

The dead bodies piled up pretty quick around Angleton, especially his wife's best friend Mary Meyer and his former friend Win Scott, the Mexico City CIA station chief who launched his own private investigation into JFK's assassination, something Angleton seemed desperate to shut down before it got started.

Since the assassination was organized through the CIA's JM/Wave station and Harvey played a key role, it's critical to consider Angleton's role in shielding Harvey after JFK ordered him removed. Shackley was running JM/Wave so he had to know what was going on, as did Helms obviously because he went on to become CIA director. In fact, if you want to know who was involved in some aspect of this coup, just consider who assumes great power in later years. Certainly the Bush family could owe a portion of its rise to prominence through a hidden connection to the coup. Shackley went on to run the Phoenix program in Vietnam with William Colby and that became the largest CIA assassination program in history. I talked to one of the key players involved a few years ago, and he told me that he'd gone back to Vietnam after the war only to discover the man in charge of providing many of the names of those who needed to be assassinated turned out to be a double agent and later became an important figure in the Vietnamese government. If that's true, then the people getting assassinated by Phoenix were probably moderate tribal leaders because once you wipe out the true alphas of any tribe, it leaves the door open to put some corrupt stooges in their place.

Maybe if you connect enough of these dots you realize why the burnt-out shell called Communism was propped in place to justify those incredible military expenditures on both sides? And why was it so easy for the CIA to whack their President but so impossible to whack Fidel Castro. Since JFK and RFK started working for world peace in 1963, one wonders if they even understood the nature of the game they were involved in. You can pick either side of the managed dialectic, but peace is never an option when your nation is run by the national security state.

The Privatization of Intelligence

If you think the prisons are being privatized, check out the secret services. Ever since Iran-Contra blew a window open on arms and drug smuggling, covert teams formerly run by the CIA started disappearing and reforming under new ownership.

The master of counter-intelligence was Angleton, and to give an idea of his operations, Jay Lovestone, the most powerful Marxist in the Labor Movement, was one of his secret agents. Angleton is now a adjective and "Angletonian" means "an overly-complex operation." To give an example, Angleton created a CIA within the CIA to keep tabs on everyone in the CIA. But then later set-up a CIA within the CIA within the CIA, in his quest to find a suspected mole at the highest levels of government, a mole he never found, unless you count his participation in the JFK assassination cover-up as the removal of the mole.

After being trained by British intelligence, Angleton started work as the Vatican connection to the CIA, but soon picked up the Israeli connection after WWII. Those two power centers are closer than you might think, and even seem to share some of the same bankers. Needless to say, British intelligence has deep connections into both. The CIA was created as a sort of merger of MI6 with Nazi and Vatican spy networks.

After the war, recently arrived Jewish immigrants into New York (people who'd been heavily traumatized and thus excellent subjects for propaganda operations) were recruited into Marxism. This was a heavily funded project and many were easily led down this path, never mind Marxism never seemed to manifest anything but fascist dictatorships, steel fists with velvet veneers.

Many of our leading universities became breeding grounds where these young Jewish Marxists were trained and indoctrinated for future roles in shaping public policy. In the late Sixties, Lyndon LaRouche trolled these grounds to build his private intelligence agency, but the John Birch Society really pioneered this privatization of intelligence. Strange how LaRouche built his network with college-age Jews while the Birchers blocked all Jews from becoming members for years, although both groups came to essentially the same conclusions on world events.

The Neo-Con movement was composed of former Marxists who'd been reconditioned for a new mission: to pave the road to war with Iraq and Afghanistan, never mind those wars nearly bankrupted our nation. Their credibility may be shot, but they still hold six-figure salaries and high positions in finance, government and the media.

Which brings me to this guy: George Friedman. *Time* magazine started promoting him in 1999. But in 2001, *Barron's* put him on the cover and ran a huge puff piece concerning his Austin-based company Statfor, supposedly the world's most effective private intelligence agency? You might wonder, who is this dude and where did he come from? (First, however, consider the messenger: *Barron's* is owned by the News Corp, part of their Dow Jones umbrella along with the *Wall Street Journal*.)

Friedman was just a lowly political science professor at Dickinson College in Pennsylvania for 20 years, but he must have been some sort of spook because he was giving national security lectures to the Army War College and Air Force's RAND. He wrote a book called "The Coming War with Japan," so he has a viable plan on keeping the war economy going just in case the phony Arab boogie-man magic show breaks down and we suddenly need to put a more powerful opponent into play.

And if that wasn't bona fides enough, along comes Wikileaks releasing a lot of Stratfor email chatter, including a conversation between Stratfor and head of security for Walmart? That must have sold a lot of companies on signing up for Stratfor's subscription service which costs $40,000 a year. That or the fact Coca-Cola was also revealed as a client.

Ken Sensor used to work for the FBI and CIA, but now he makes big bucks for Walmart. You know the anti-Walmart websites? Sensor runs some of those because he's a well-trained spook in the post-Angleton era, and knows the value of counter-intelligence operations. So he has sock puppets on both sides of the divide. Anyway, a Walmart employee in Mexico got a threatening email demanding removal of a new security measure on the website or watch your relatives start dying. Sensor sent the threat, written in Spanish, to Stratfor and got the following response:

Subject: Re: CONFIDENTIAL – Question Regarding Gulf Cartel

Ken –Our initial read –The Spanish grammar and spelling is similar to that used by the Gulf Cartel and Los Zetas, however the excessive use of the 'z' leads me to believe it might have been Los Zetas, but that is more a personal hunch than any pictures or other messages I have seen. Have not heard of this email address or tactic before. There are a lot of bad guys posing as Zetas or Gulf, just for the fear factor, and it could be just some posers. One aspect to consider is narco taxes. Perhaps this person owes money or narco taxes for protection? There is no business in MX untouched by this. If your folks aren't telling Hqs about it, it would not surprise me.

--Fred

If you've been following my research, you know I think Wikileaks is an Angletonian-style project and strongly suspect this Wikileaks/Stratfor connection is just a window on the dynamics of building deep intelligence operations. Notice this email actually contains zero useful information, and one wonders why Wikileaks even thinks this is a "leak" of anything at all.

Last year, Max Fisher wrote an amusing story in the *Atlantic* titled: "Stratfor is a Joke and so is Wikileaks for Taking It Seriously." Fisher characterized their subscription service as "getting *The Economist* a week later and several hundred times more expensive."

Nomenclature of the Octopus Cabal

"What is history but a fable agreed upon?"
—Napoleon Bonaparte

\

Major historical events, such as revolution, assassination and war, are usually presented as random events created through chaos and chance. Should any suggest these seminal events are more likely the result of plots hatched in secret, they are quickly dismissed as conspiracy-theory crackpots. Yet anyone who studies the difficulties of absorbing and maintaining power soon understands it's far more likely that war and political assassination are the result of hidden conspiracies than random incidents involving isolated loners.

Many would agree that 9/11 was perpetrated by the world's biggest illegal drug cartel. The only question remaining is who exactly runs that cartel? If food and energy are the world's biggest profit streams, generating trillions per year in revenues, illegal drugs may not be far behind. More important, illegal drugs represent the world's largest cash economy, bigger than Walmart. The little-known secret of banking is that some banks depend on this cash to survive, and, in fact, the system can dry up and blow away if major sources of liquidity are suddenly removed. But it wasn't always this way. To understand the depth of corruption in today's banking industry and the systemic use of black market funds, it's useful to have some background in banking history, something few Americans seem to possess. Let's follow the yellow brick road, shall we?

Denarius of Marus Aurelelius

Around 300 BC, the Roman Republic established the first global currency in the form of metal coins stamped with the image of notable Roman faces. Gold and silver are minted in Rome, while bronze and copper are minted around the empire. The system worked remarkably well for nearly eight centuries. But after Rome gradually drained all silver out of its "silver" coin, inflation set in and its western empire collapsed, opening the door for a new global banking authority.

Founded in 1119 with only nine members, The Knights Templar was a religious order granted a Papal exemption from usury. This highly secretive order began operations by generating "letters of credit" for pilgrims traveling to the Holy Land. The letters evolve into a check-writing system and the Templars grow into a force of 20,000. They maintain a private army, navy, forts, merchant ships, and intelligence network, and build Europe's greatest cathedrals (some of which contain magic mushroom iconography). For two centuries the Templars effectively become the world's central bank as they hold large repositories of gold and are the investment bank of choice for European royalty looking to initiate wars of conquest. The King of France falls deeply in their debt.

In 1198, another society appeared out of Germany, also recognized by the Pope of Rome, the *Order of Brothers of the German House of Saint Mary in Jerusalem*, otherwise known as the Teutonic Knights, and they go on to establish the kingdom of Prussia. After the Templars became the most powerful global corporation, and began making plans to establish their own kingdom in southern France in imitation of the Teutonic Knights, the French King devised a plot to move the Papacy to France in order to outlaw the order and seize its assets, while killing or imprisoning most known members. The secret operation unfolds on Friday the 13th in 1307, which is why Friday the 13th has magical connotations today.

The Templars and Teutonics created initiatory societies with secret rituals and degrees, all under the direction of a grandmaster of the order, typically a position held for life. These magical societies had obviously been influenced by the Pythagoreans who had enjoyed immense popularity before the Catholic Church began persecuting paganism. Pythagoras studied with Zoroastrians, the greatest mathematicians and astronomers, and the Zoroastrians had been influenced by the Scythians, and adopted their sacramental and inspirational use of cannabis. All the original knight myths (as well as the story of the holy grail) can be traced to a Scythian influence. King Arthur is merely an update on Heracles.

After the Templars were roasted alive at the stake, various secret societies flourished all over Europe, the most powerful became known as Freemasonry. The oldest-known masonic lodge is in Scotland and traces its order to 1598, although masonry could have been established as early as 1425. There was some speculation at the time that the Templars might have slipped into masonry in order to survive.

In 1400 the Medici Bank in Florence, Italy, invented double-entry bookkeeping and became the world's biggest bank for generations, famous for persecuting Jews and murder plots against other banking families in Italy, a country where banking reigned supreme for several more centuries. The Jewish del Bancos become a dominant banking family in Venice until forced to flee to Warburg, Germany.

In the 1500s, Holy Roman Emperor Charles V of Spain institutionalizes fractional reserve banking, which means banks are allowed to loan more money than they have on deposit, thereby creating new money as debt. This becomes the bankers' favorite tool for generating profits and controlling money supply, which, in turn, leads to booms and busts.

In 1534, seven Spanish noblemen with military backgrounds establish the *Society of Jesus*, known as the Jesuits, and this order assumed fantastic power, eclipsing even the mighty Templars, at which point the Jesuits began attracting persecutions all over Europe, starting in Portugal. Paranoia against them became so great eventually the Pope outlawed the order in 1773, and they fled to sanctuary in Russia for a few years while still managing to hold onto many assets through fronting operations.

Two years later, the *Equestrian, Secular and Chapterial Order of Saint Joachim* was established in Bavaria by 14 German nobles. Some were Catholic, some Lutheran, some Freemasons, some Rosicrucians. Their possible goal was the unification of Germany, which was splintered into 500 separate kingdoms. These knights were dedicated to spreading religious tolerance. It doesn't take much imagination to realize that tolerance might include letting the Jesuits back into Europe. Germany had been divided between Lutherans and Catholics for centuries, resulting in almost constant warfare, so religious tolerance was a popular concept.

The following year after the appearance of the Joachim knights, the *Covenant of Perfectibility* was created at a Jesuit-owned university in Bavaria by a professor of Catholic law named Adam Weishaupt, an orphan raised by Jesuits. The name of Weishaupt's group was eventually changed to *Order of the Illuminati*. Several Knights of Joachim were founding members, which certainly guaranteed tremendous influence and potential resources. Weishaupt was a master counterintelligence strategist, and his society was designed as a secret nest inside Freemasonry.

"The great strength of our Order lies in its concealment," wrote Weishaupt, "let it never appear in any place in its own name, but always covered by another name, and another occupation. None is fitter than the three lower degrees of Freemasonry, the public is accustomed to it, expects little from it, and therefore takes little notice of it. Next to this, the form of a learned or literary society is best suited to our purpose. By establishing Reading Societies, and subscription libraries, and taking these under our direction, and supplying them through our labours, we may turn the public mind which way we will."

Weishaupt suggested they secretly enlist the most attractive members of the opposite sex possible into the operation, not as full-fledged members but as secret operatives, what's known today in spook world as "honey traps."

Weishaupt sought virtuous and non-virtuous members, and kept those two groups unaware of the other. In fact, most members only knew their handler, and once a person joined, Weishaupt was given details on their background, desires and ambitions, and some were immediately elevated, guaranteeing their lifelong devotion to his order. The Templars, Teutonics, and Jesuits had pioneered the art of counterintelligence, and Weishaupt may have studied them all. But he had no background in ritual, and launched his society prematurely with a plethora of degrees before he had any rituals on paper. He reached out to an experienced mason to invent the rituals.

When some of Weishaupt's methods were revealed to the public, there was a panic against secret societies in Bavaria and all were outlawed, although the ban was repeated several times, indicating it had a slippery hold on the situation and it's possible the ban only served to make the group more notorious and more popular, just as it's possible Weishaupt was a Jesuit front all along. Eventually, Weishaupt announced the dissolution of the order and retired to live near the estate of one of the Joachim Knights.

But after the French revolution, the leading Jesuit in France declared the Jacobins who fomented the revolution had been manipulated by the Illuminati, a charge repeated by a Christian historian in Scotland. In fact, various reading rooms around France had helped foment the revolution, just as Weishaupt had suggested they do.

Europe in the 17th and 18th centuries was a dangerous place for progressive ideas. The continent festered with secret police and informants. Inquisitions and pogroms could be convened at any moment to deal with rabble-rousers who threatened the status quo. Secret societies developed as a result of this persecution. "Liberty, equality, and fraternity" were the principles of revolts that swept through Holland, North America, France, and the Masonic secret societies.

Masonic lodges became the primary incubators of revolutionary thought because most carried no dogmas, allowing lodges to create and interpret ritual through their own consensus. They also allowed people of different religions and backgrounds to mingle freely as equals. Consequently, Freemasonry was able to morph as it spread through Europe and North America. But it always maintained a pyramidal structure that allowed a small upper cell to conduct intrigues not revealed to the general membership.

"Because of the increasing effectiveness of the political police, secret societies tended to move even further underground," writes James H. Billington in *Fire in the Mind of Men: Origins of the Revolutionary Faith.* "Historians have never been able to unravel the tangled threads of this of this tapestry—and in recent times have largely given up trying. The most important recent study confines itself to tracing the history of what people thought about secret societies rather than what the societies in fact were.... The story of secret societies can never fully be reconstructed, but it has been badly neglected—even avoided, one suspects—because the evidence that is available repeatedly leads us into territory equally uncongenial to modern historians in the East and West.

Hell-Fire

The oldest still-existing Masonic lodge was established in Edinburgh on July 3, 1600, a year that also saw the creation of the East India Company, a firm that would become infamous for opium running and slave trading. For centuries the East India Company would be closely linked to British intelligence and Freemasonry. In 1664, Edinburgh Lodge No. 1 admitted Lord Alexander and two other nobles. English royalty would eventually dominate the upper rungs of British Freemasonry.

In 1600, prominent British families banded together to create a cartel known as the British East India Company (a pioneering multinational corporation). Like the Templars, this company will eventually maintain its own armies, forts and conquered lands. The East India Company trades in cotton, silk and tea, but the biggest profit-maker is opium, although to maximize profits it must be smuggled into China, where black-market prices prevail.

The Bank of Amsterdam is created in 1609 and becomes the only bank whose charter demands a 100% reserve, a system that lasts for 170 years. During this period, Amsterdam becomes the trading capital of the world.

The Bank of England is created in 1694 and immediately becomes Britain's central bank and the model for which all future central banks will be created. It is a private bank with an exclusive government contract. In 1717, Sir Isaac Newton establishes a mint ratio that devalues silver, putting England on the gold standard.

In 1700, the first public leaflets warning the populace abut the dangers of Freemasonry appeared in London. In 1719, two years after Freemasonry went above ground (and all lodges organized around a central Grand Lodge), the Hell Fire Club was created by two prominent Freemasons, the Duke of Wharton and the Earl of

Litchfield. Devoted to debauchery and sinful activities of pleasure, Hell Fire Clubs spread throughout England, Scotland and Ireland, exclusive secret societies for those of noble birth. The Dublin chapter was organized by the Earl of Rosse, who would later be named Grand Master of Ireland's Freemasons. The clubs became notorious for recreational drug use, black masses and orgies.

Although the Hell Fire Clubs were officially condemned by the Grand Lodge (as well as the English churches), the fact that the Duke of Wharton was named Grand Master of the English Grand Lodge in 1722 reveals there may have been a hidden connection all along. The duke would also introduce Freemasonry to Spain and later become Grand Master of French Freemasonry. Did the public emergence of Freemasonry demand the creation of new secret societies submerged from public view?

Anti-Masonic sentiments first erupted when the Society of Gormogons appeared in London. Outspoken critics of Freemasonry, the Gormogons claimed the Emperor of China as their founder and the czar of Russia as their most powerful initiate. Disaffected Freemasons were encouraged to burn their aprons and gloves and become Gormogons. Strangely, the Duke of Wharton was a prominent member as well. And thus begins the saga of the anti-Masonic groups, some of which seem to have been secretly controlled by Freemasons. (One must always keep in mind that the creation and manipulation of two sides of a conflict would become standard operating procedure for secret societies.)

According to *Holy Bood, Holy Grail* by Michael Baigent, Henry Lincoln, and Richard Leigh, the highest initiates of British Freemasonry are taught that Jesus was king of Britain and that he was stoned to death at the location of St. Paul's Cathedral. While Jesus' evil twin brother, Judas Thomas, was killed by the Romans, the true Jesus sought refuge in England where he learned the secrets of the Druids, married four women, and produced many children. The current Prince of Wales is a direct descendant, as are much of Europe's royalty. While this fanciful story may seem ridiculous, no doubt it was taken seriously by a few royal Freemasons, since it firmly establishing their divine right to rule. And no doubt a few may even still believe this myth today.

Revolution and Rothschilds

No history of banking would be complete without extensive mention of the Rothschild dynasty. Mayer Rothschild had the brilliant idea to relocate his sons to five banking centers in Europe and carefully spread their wealth around to protect it from the sort of seizure that destroyed the Templars. Austria granted royal titles to several lines of the family and eventually a Rothschild became the first Jew admitted to the English House of Lords.

In 1790, Mayer Amschel Bauer was an anonymous merchant specializing in rare coins and antiques who lived in the crowded ghetto in Frankfurt, the banking hub of Germany. Ten years later, he was one of the richest men in Germany. Whenever one finds such a meteoric rise to wealth, the potential influence of secret societies needs to be examined.

Bauer had a powerful patron in Wilhelm IV, reportedly one of the leading royal masons of his day. In fact, Jewish culture became an inseparable part of masonic traditions from the beginning. Because Jews were exempt from the Vatican ban on usury, they could be helpful in waging war or establishing monopolies in commerce. Many masonic rituals seem taken from the pages of the Kabala, a school of Jewish mysticism some scholars trace back to year 1. Some historians even believe Pythagoras received his training from the Kabala, and Pythagorean numerology played a major role in the occult rituals of secret societies during the

179

Revolutionary period. According to Jacob Katz's *Jews and Freemasons in Europe, 1723-1939*, the Rothschilds began appearing on masonic membership lists in 1811. "Special Jewish lodges were created," writes Katz, "such as the 'Melchizedek' lodges, named in honor of the Old Testament priest-king."

The Rothschild dynasty has also been suspected of being a major supporter of Grand Orient Freemasonry, a primary incubator of the French Revolution, which ultimately brought Napoleon into power. Napoleon's membership in the Grand Orient was never proven, but his brothers and sons all became initiates. Napoleon's island home, Corsica, has a long history of conspiratorial activity, as does Sicily.

Grand Orient Masonry had the same codes, secret handshakes and rituals as English Masonry. In fact, members of either organization were always welcome at each other's ceremonies, which made masonic lodges an ideal setting for spy activities. French masonry was the more rational, since it permitted atheists to join. In Germany, however, the masonic movement went in the opposite direction, becoming more magical and occult-based. German masonry was also mixed with elements of the secret Rosicrucian Brotherhood, which claimed access to secrets of the East and an unbroken chain of grandmasters almost as long as the Templars.

As the story of secret societies unfolds, a pattern becomes clear. Whenever a new lodge or branch of masonry was created, there was an attempt to create a fictional history linking the new society to the Crusades or biblical times. Napoleon went even further. After conquering Egypt, he became initiated into an Egyptian secret society supposedly older that the Templars. Or was this just another Masonic spin-off trick?

Meanwhile, during a trip to England, Benjamin Franklin was asked why the Colonies seemingly have no unemployed while mother England is full of homeless beggars. He replied: "In the Colonies, we issue our own paper money. It is called 'Colonial Scrip.' We control its purchasing power and we have no interest to pay to no one." This comes as a surprise to the British bankers who quickly demand Colonial Scrip be outlawed, cutting the Colonial money supply in half, which creates extreme hardship. According to Franklin, this is the real trigger for the American Revolution, not a relatively insignificant tax on tea. Franklin would later be unmasked as a British spy.

Not long after the Revolutionary War, in 1785, the US adopted a silver standard based on the Spanish milled dollar. The biggest controversy of the new nation concerned whether to establish a privately held central bank. Alexander Hamilton (founder of the Bank of New York) lobbied for it, while Thomas Jefferson argued strongly against it. Hamilton won and the first Bank of the United States was created in 1792. Public outcry was so great, however, it dissolved in 1811.

Meanwhile, the Rothschilds become masters of "pump and dump" and other legal methods for swindling the masses. After creating and crashing economic bubbles, bankers purchase assets for pennies on the dollar. The Rothschilds gain significant power after the Battle of Waterloo by spreading rumors of a Napoleonic victory, which creates an exploitable financial panic. Soon, their bank is famous for funding both sides of war simultaneously.

The 2nd Bank of the United States is created in 1816 by President James Madison and lasts until 1833, when it is killed by President Andrew Jackson. There is no more central bank in the USA for 73 years and Jackson will always consider killing the central bank his greatest achievement.

In 1832, The Order of Skull and Bones is created at Yale University. It is the first American branch of an elite German secret society. Many of the original members come from families involved with the opium trade. Bonesmen quickly gravitate to the pinnacles of power in finance, government, education, publishing and military intelligence.

In 1857 a banking panic spreads through North America as the economy sours and several banks fail. This collapse becomes a contributing factor to the Civil War. Former Torys who'd supported England during the Revolutionary War (located around Boston and New York) emerge as among the country's richest families and quietly fund the abolitionist movement (including terrorists like John Brown, whose goal is to spark a violent confrontation). Unfortunately, President Abraham Lincoln goes along with the war plans (rather than resist secession non-violently). But Lincoln refuses to borrow money to finance the war since banks demand over 20% interest. So Lincoln prints his own debt-free paper money (greenbacks).

After the war, J.P. Morgan emerges as the dominant financial power in North America due to his war profiteering off defective weapons. But Morgan will not stand alone: Rockefeller, Carnegie, Mellon, and many other names from the Social Register make fortunes during and after the Civil War, and almost all are devoted anglophiles with deep connections to British banks.

England is on the gold standard and the United States remains on a bimetallic standard (gold and silver). But in 1873, in what becomes known as the "Crime of 73," Congress demonetizes silver, resulting in a gold-to-silver ratio shift of 16-1 to 40-1. In 1886, William Jennings Bryan runs for President, campaigning to end American imperialism, restore a bimetallic standard, and give women the vote. His opponent, William McKinley, is the approved candidate of Wall Street. Bryan becomes known as "the lion," for his fiery speeches, so McKinley brands him a "cowardly lion" on account of his opposition to war. Bryan might have won but a sudden rise in the value of crops causes farmers to switch allegiance before the election. The Wizard of Oz is an allegory for this famous struggle. In the original book, Dorothy wears silver slippers, the key to defeating the evil witch. The Cowardly Lion falling asleep in a poppy field is likely a reference to Bryan's devotion to Christianity. According to Karl Marx, religion is the opium of the masses, and nothing represents opium like a field of poppies. Bryan ends his career with a long, protracted battle against the theory of evolution.

In 1871, the privately held Reichsbank becomes the central bank of the newly created German empire, replacing 31 separate Prussian central banks, all of whom had been issuing money. The highly stable Goldmark is born.

Aside from the Jesuits, the Vatican had a military order under its command, known as the Hospitallers of St. John of Jerusalem. Naturally, this order traced its origins to an earlier date than the Templars. They became known as the Knights of Rhodes in 1309 and have been called the Knights of Malta since 1530, according to their Internet site. However, the Malta Knights seem to have inspired some Masonic-style organizations, most of which are not recognized by the Vatican. The most infamous lodge was created after Napoleon invaded Malta. This order sought refuge in Russia and later, after the Russian Revolution, in Pennsylvania. Although branded as a "false order" by the Pope, the Shickshinny Knights of Malta of Pennsylvania are legendary for their far-right political activities, as well as for having British and Russian nobility in their membership.

Weishaupt was one of the only secret society leaders ever accused of plotting world domination, in a trial that created reverberations in Masonic lodges around the world. A Bavarian court outlawed the Illuminati (and all other secret societies) in 1785, but most historians believe the highly publicized trial only drove the organizations deeper underground. Today, many researchers understand the importance of Freemasonry in the American Revolution. The Boston Tea Party was organized out of the St. Andrew's Lodge, of which Paul Revere was a member. Revere would later become Grand Master of Massachusetts. George Washington was Grand Master of Virginia, and 33 of his generals were reportedly members, as were the two most prominent nobles arriving from Europe to assist with the Revolution, Marquis de Lafayette and Baron von Steuben. Technically, the American lodges were supposed to separate from their British associations during the war, although the majority of members undoubtedly supported the English king and not the revolution.

Masons and Mormons

One of the more interesting episodes in masonic history concerns the simultaneous creation of the short-lived Anti-Masonic Party and the long-lived and now immensely powerful Church of Jesus Christ of Latter-Day Saints, or Mormon church.

After retired Captain William Morgan signed a contract with the publisher of the Advocate of Batavia, New York to write an expose on Freemasonry he was arrested, kidnapped from his jail cell on September 19, 1826, and taken to Canada, where he disappeared. His manuscript, *Illustrations of Masonry*, was published in his absence, with all proceeds going to his wife, since it was presumed Morgan had been murdered by Masons.

With all the publicity surrounded Morgan's disappearance, *Illustrations of Masonry* led to the creation of the Anti-Masonic Party, the first third party in the United States. This new party grew rapidly, electing members to national office, and campaigning under the belief that masonry was controlled by

European aristocrats, working with old Tory families in a royalist plot to take back America. Today, the brief Anti-Masonic party is best known for creating the first political convention featuring open voting on candidates. The party also created the first national party platform, and required candidates to support it.

On September 22, 1827, Freemason Joseph Smith claimed to have been visited by an angel named Moroni, who directed him to uncover some golden tablets buried near Palmyra, New York. These tablets became the basis for the Mormon religion, a modern-day recreation of the Moses legend, sans any burning bushes. Due to hostility to both Masonry and Mormonism, which share similarities in ritual and secrecy, Smith was forced to move his lodges west, first to Ohio, then to Nauvoo, Illinois.

The story took an event stranger twist when William Morgan's widow, Lucinda, married Freemason George W. Harris on November 23, 1830, which just happened to be the same year Smith founded the Mormon Church in a nearby New York town. The couple moved to Nauvoo and converted to Mormonism, leaving some to wonder if the entire Morgan affair had not been stage-managed for some hidden purpose. No doubt royalties on Morgan's book helped fund the church's relocation to Utah.

Antagonism toward the Morgan/Mason lodges in Illinois was so intense that a neighboring town decided to invade Nauvoo, with the intention of killing Smith and his followers. At the same time, Smith was being held in protective custody in jail. A mob descended upon the jail and murdered Smith as he displayed the secret masonic sign of distress in a failed bid for mercy. Both Masonry and Mormonism were born in blood.

The Mormons moved on without Smith to found Council Bluffs, Iowa, a key strategic point for crossing the Missouri River into Nebraska, and what would later become Salt Lake City, where they created a new state (Utah) founded on Mormon principles. Located near their grand temple is an almost equally grand Masonic temple built around the same time.

Masonry continued to leverage astonishing power in North America. In fact, the Civil War may have been a masonic plot to divide and conquer the country. The Rothschilds, who had departed Germany to take up primary residence in London, loaned money to both sides during the war, and British agents of the East India Company helped foment antagonisms. Bostonian Albert Pike rapidly ascended to the leadership of American Freemasonry and became a general of the Confederacy, charged with enlisting the help of Native Americans in joining the South, as well as participating in the Knights of the Golden Circle and the Ku Klux Klan.

President Lincoln rejected the outrageous interest demanded by European banks, and began producing a national currency know as "greenbacks," which replaced dozens of private currencies being used as any bank could issue its own money before the Civil War, but not after. (When President Kennedy would revive the Greenback many years later, it was an attempt to reign in the Central Bank, not create it.) But after Lincoln was assassinated by a plot inside his own government that left him unprotected while a Confederate Secret Agent fired a single-shot derringer, President Andrew Johnson, a devoted Freemason, pardoned Albert Pike for any war crimes he committed by organizing Natives to commit acts of terror against Northern towns. But when Johnson later tried to retire War Department chief Edwin M. Stanton, an impeachment effort was immediately launched against Johnson, while Stanton barricaded himself in his office until the trial was over. Stanton's power had grown immensely after Lincoln's death, and he wanted control over his Lincoln assassination files, which would be kept secret for another hundred years.

Albert Pike would go on to re-write the book on Freemasonry, replacing three degrees with thirty-three, and his 11-foot bronze statue stands proudly at Third and D Streets in downtown Washington, D.C., although few outside masonry know who he is. The statue has been owned and maintained by the National Parks Service since its placement was mandated by a joint session of Congress on April 9, 1898.

Skull & Bones

In 1833, William H. Russell and Alphonso Taft created an elite secret society at Yale University that has become known as Skull & Bones, after an emblem used in its rituals. Most of what we know about the society comes from the work of the late Antony C. Sutton, former research fellow at the Hoover Institute of Stanford University.

In 1968, Sutton published *Western Technology and Soviet Economic Development*, a book that documented enormous technological transfers between the United States and the Soviet Union. Sutton proved that Russia at the end of World War II was a backward, bombed-out shell of a country, and her rise to international power was accomplished only through hidden assistance from the US. When Sutton promised to continue his research, he was fired from the Hoover Institute and warned not to "break his rice bowl." Sutton would go on to write 26 books detailing the corruption of US financial, medical, educational, and political systems. Although these books would sell tens of thousands of copies, none would ever be reviewed in any newspaper in America.

As Harvard Professor Richard Pipes wrote in Survival Is Not Enough: Soviet Realities and America's Future, "Sutton comes to conclusions that are uncomfortable for many businessmen and economists. For this reason his work tends to be either dismissed out of hand as 'extreme' or, more often, simply ignored."

Sutton suspected a secret cabal was orchestrating events behind the curtain, but the key to unlocking the identity of a major component of the system did not arrive until the early Eighties, when he received a letter asked if he would care to examine the membership list of Skull & Bones. "It was a black bag job was a family member disgusted by their activities," wrote Sutton. The membership list arrived in two volumes, black-leather bound. Living members and deceased members were listed in separate volumes. "I kept the stack of Xerox sheets for quite a while before I looked at them," recalled Sutton. "When I did look—a picture jumped out: this was a significant part of the so-called establishment."

As Sutton investigated the apparatus, he was shocked to discover that the society had played important roles in funding the rise of the Nazis, as well as assisting the Russian Revolution, which had been organized primarily through masonic lodges in Switzerland, England, and Russia. Since Skull & Bones was a chapter of a German-based secret society based on the philosophical principles of Georg W.F. Hegel, with its oppositional dialectic, Sutton soon began documenting how war and revolution had been manipulated for profit. Although Skull & Bones was dominated by old-money families, two new-money families—the Harrimans and the Rockefellers, respective patriarchs of the Democratic and Republican parties—had taken on important roles.

Near the end of World War II, the occult and masonic-styled Nazi SS secretly surrendered to Dulles in Operation Sunrise. The massive transfer of Nazi war criminals to safety in North and South America was handled with the assistance of the Vatican, and the Knights of Malta. Churches became sanctuaries for Nazi spies and scientists, many of whom would end up inside the newly created American Gestapo, the CIA, with Dulles was placed in charge. Not only was Hitler's intelligence chief, Reinhardt Gehlen, a Malta Knight, but so was Dulles and many highly placed members of US military intelligence. The Nazis who were spirited away to safety included experts in rocket science, torture and mind control. Brainwashing had been a major field of study at the concentration camps, and the results of these grisly experiments had obviously been deemed of important national interest.

In 1910, Nelson Aldrich is one of the most powerful politicians in America, head of the Republican Party and chairman of the Senate Finance Committee. His daughter Abby is married to John D. Rockefeller Jr. Aldrich organizes a secret meeting at a private club on Jekyll Island favored by the Morgans and Vanderbilts. The meeting includes Paul Warburg, (Kuhn & Loeb), Frank Vanderlip (National City Bank of New York), Henry P. Davison (J.P. Morgan), Charles Norton (First National Bank of New York) and Benjamin Strong (J.P. Morgan). Together, they represent one fourth of the world's wealth. Warburg is the primary architect of a plan for a private banking cartel and central bank. Later that year, an orchestrated financial panic and economic depression occurs following the enforcement of the Sherman Anti-Trust Act, and in 1911, The Supreme Court breaks up Standard Oil, at the time the largest corporation in the world. The Federal Reserve Act is passed on December 23, 1913, while most of Congress is on holiday. It is hyped as protection against future depressions, but some Congressmen are not fooled and know the country has been handed over to a private banking cartel. That same year, J.P. Morgan dies and Rockefeller establishes a foundation to shelter his immense fortune from taxes.

Hamburg banker Max Warburg (brother of Paul) becomes chief adviser to the German Kaiser Wilhelm II at the start of World War I. The war is billed as "the war to end all wars." Meanwhile, in 1915, the Robber Barons pool their funds to create the America International Corporation (AIC). United Fruit is just one of hundreds of companies AIC will control. Czar Nicolas II abdicates following the February Revolution in Russia. Germany and Wall Street back exiled Bolsheviks to return to Russia to subvert a democracy that has spontaneously emerged to replace the Czar. In April, the US enters WWI. Six months later, the fully-funded October Counter-Revolution sweeps Lenin into power. Later evidence indicates Lenin and the Bolsheviks receive essential support from Germany and Wall Street to finance this coup.

In 1925 I.G. Farben is formed through the merger of six major corporations in Germany and instantly becomes the dominant corporation of Europe, referred to as "the cartel." The company is designed by John Foster Dulles and based on the operations of Standard Oil. It is the fourth largest corporation in the world, behind only General Motors, U.S. Steel and the downsized Standard Oil. Max Warburg is one of the directors.

In 1928, the Federal Reserve begins raising interest rates to slow market speculation and one year later, Wall Street crashes, creating the Great Depression. Few seem to recall the Federal Reserve had been created supposedly to prevent such an event.

The Bank for International Settlements (BIS) is formed in Basel, Switzerland, in 1930, ostensibly to facilitate German war reparations, but actually BIS is designed to function as a central bank to the privately-held central banks. Participating countries are required to stockpile gold in Basel (supposedly the world's largest supply after Fort Knox) and this gold is used to settle debts between nations. By international treaty, the BIS is immune from governmental interference or taxation and can never be audited. From its inception, the leadership of BIS is dominated by powerful Nazis who have just assumed control of Germany.

190

In 1934, two-time Congressional Medal of Honor winner Major General Smedley Butler tries to blow the whistle on a Wall Street plot to remove President Franklin Roosevelt and establish a military dictatorship. Butler pretends to go along with this plot in order to identify the major sponsors and then presents the evidence to an embarrassed Congress, who immediately goes into private session and circles the wagons to protect the guilty. According to Butler, return of the recently abandoned gold standard is a major objective of the coup. Butler is ridiculed, the plotters exonerated. The following year, Butler publishes War is a Racket, a devastating condemnation of Wall Street imperialism. He dies unexpectedly five years later at age 59 and few Americans ever read the book or even know his name.

I. G. Farben becomes a major sponsor and chief corporate cheerleader for Adolf Hitler's conquests. At the start of the war, the company holds more shares of Standard Oil than any other entity except the Rockefeller family. They will produce all Zyklon B used in concentration camps. Strangely, many Wall Street companies conduct business with Germany throughout the war, most notably Standard Oil. The Luftwaffe, in fact, is dependent on fuel from Standard Oil throughout the duration of the war. Some of this activity is arranged secretly through the BIS. Hitler's first act after invading any country is confiscation of gold reserves, including all gold at the BIS, which is dutifully transferred to the Reichsbank.

After the D-Day invasion, a "bridge too far" is kept open near the Netherlands-German border, possibly to allow gold shipments out of Germany into safe havens in Holland. Immediately after the war, American forces headquarter at Farben while hundreds of Nazi war criminals, scientists and intelligence operatives are disappeared into North and South America. Those that remain in Europe are recruited into a secret stay-behind network (Gladio) to foment terror operations during the Cold War. The bulk of Nazi spy operations are morphed into the newly-created CIA. According to former SS Commander Paul Hausser, the foreign divisions of the Nazi SS become the foundation for NATO..

During the war Germans and Japanese steal gold now worth trillions, almost all of which disappears. Much of the German gold is washed through the BIS, while the Japanese gold is recovered slowly from booby-trapped burial sites in the Phillipines. Military intelligence operative Paul Helliwell is involved in the recovery. The gold is washed through dozens of banks to conceal its origin and placed into hundreds of secret accounts used to support a Wall Street agenda around the globe for the next sixty years, an inexhaustible slush fund for dirty tricks. Completely cloaked through national security, this "Black Eagle Fund" is devised and orchestrated by Henry Stimson, member of the Yale's Skull & Bones. In 1951, Helliwell sets up the Sea Supply Corporation to provide weapons to Taiwan and Thailand. The company immediately becomes involved with opium.

In 1952, the Reece Committee on Tax Exempt Foundations is created by Congress to investigate corporate foundation support of communism. Banker Norman Dodd is appointed chief investigator and will eventually conclude the Rockefeller, Ford and Carnegie Foundations are weakening individualism in order to allow central government to assume greater power. Privately, Ford Foundation President H. Rowan Gaither informs Dodd the foundation heads have experience with intelligence operations and are under directives from the White House to "use grant-making power to alter life in the United States so that it can be comfortably merged with the Soviet Union." Gaither will later deny making the comment. According to Dodd, the investigation is confronted with "obstacles and interference at every turn."

In June, 1963, President Kennedy instructs his Treasury Secretary to issue $4 billion in debt-free silver certificates. JFK plans to end the oil depletion allowance and "break the CIA into a thousand pieces." David Rockefeller writes an op-ed in the *New York Times* blasting JFK's policies. Kennedy will be dead in a few months.

Paul Helliwell meeting Michael Hand and Frank Nugan.

In 1964, Helliwell creates the Castle Bank in Freeport, The Bahamas, although the bank doesn't become operational for another three years. It will soon become the bank of choice for the CIA and organized crime, especially Meyer Lansky. An IRS investigation into the bank is quickly shut down, but not before the CIA-mafia connections are revealed. The bank is gutted and goes belly up..

In 1973, Nugan Hand Ltd is founded in Sidney, Australia, by an Australian mobster and a former Green Beret involved in the opium trade. It will become the CIA and mafia's favorite bank for many years following the demise of Castle Bank. Nugan Hand creates branches around the globe run by retired high-ranking military officers. When a scandal breaks out regarding the bank's involvement in Australian politics, Frank Nugan is murdered and Michael Hand vanishes. According to the official Australian investigation, Nugan Hand financed a secret war in Laos with drug money and sold weapons illegally around the world, among many other crimes.

The Bank of Credit and Commerce International (BCCI) was registered in Luxembourg by a Pakistani financier in 1972. But after the fall of Nugan Hand, it quickly becomes the 7th largest private bank in the world with 400 branches in 78 countries. BCCI is heavily involved with the CIA and organized crime in money laundering, drug running, illegal arms sales, and terrorism. The bank also supports CIA operations in Afghanistan.

In 1980, Charlotte Iserbyt, Senior Policy Advisor in the Office of Educational Research, has a chance encounter with Norman Dodd and becomes so upset with corruption of the education system that she publishes *The Deliberate Dumbing Down of America*. Iserbyt leaks her father's Skull & Bones membership directory to economist Antony Sutton, who has been exposing Wall Street connections to Nazi Germany and the Soviet Union. Sutton will use the list to write his most important book, *America's Secret Establishment*. It is the most articulate analysis of Wall Street's secret agenda ever written and will never be reviewed in any newspaper in America.

In 1982, CIA Director William Casey gets a legal exemption sparing any members of the CIA from reporting on drug smuggling by CIA officers, agents, or assets. Attorney General William French Smith grants the exemption in a secret memorandum.

After Barry Seal threatens to blow the whistle on CIA drug smuggling, he is murdered in Baton Rouge, Louisiana, in 1986. Seal flew planes for the Medellin Cartel, but was really undercover with the CIA and DEA. He is murdered by the cartel after Lt. Colonel Oliver North reveals his work as an informant in the Iran-Contra Hearings, controlled by Bonesman John Kerry.

In 1988, Pan Am 103 blew up over Scotland. The plane carries four intelligence agents returning to Washington DC to blow the whistle on controlled deliveries of heroin out of the Beka Valley. Pan Am learns this after hiring former Mossad agent Juval Aviv to investigate the incident.

In 1990, Pete Brewton of the *Houston Post* uncovers evidence linking the CIA and mafia to looting dozens of Savings & Loans over the previous decade. No national media picks up his fully-documented story. The bailout of the failed Savings & Loans eventually cost the taxpayers over $153 billion (more than the Vietnam War).

In 1991, after the British media reports BCCI is providing arms to Iran and funding terrorists, the bank is forced to close and liquidate (75% of assets are eventually recovered). The bank pays $10 million in fines and forfeits $550 million in American assets, most of which is simply redistributed to shareholders. It goes down as the largest forfeiture in history. Danny Casolaro, an investigative reporter researching BCCI, Pan Am 103, Iran Contra, and other scandals, is found dead in Martinsburg, West Virginia. His family is shocked when the body is immediately embalmed without permission and the death ruled a suicide. Casolaro had developed a theory of a secret mafia inside the government involved in arms trading and illegal drugs. He called them "the Octopus" because of their connections to the JFK assassination, Watergate and Iran Contra.

In 1996, investigative reporter Gary Webb publishes evidence linking the spread of crack in Los Angeles to the CIA's contra supply network. He is crucified in the media and loses his journalism career. Although no one will ever disprove a single fact, Webb later commits suicide after defaulting on his mortgage.

In 1999, Alexander Hamilton's prestigious Bank of New York was discovered laundering billions for Semen Mogilevich, the Meyer Lansky of Russia. The bank eventually pays a paltry $38 million to settle two criminal probes against it, although the Russian government later sues for $22.5 billion. At the time, the case is dubbed "the biggest financial scandal of all time," but not a single member of the bank's executive staff is indicted. A lowly clerk who lies about her compensation package spends one week in jail after pleading guilty. The Federal Reserve inflicts no fine nor penalty and the bank's stock never wavers during many trials and investigations, most of which are mysteriously dropped. Court records reveal interaction between bank executives, organized crime, massive worldwide fraud, drug and weapon trafficking, and murder-for-hire. Billions transferred through the International Monetary Fund and intended for Russia remain unaccounted for.

On September 10th, 2001, Donald Rumsfeld went on national television to admit the Pentagon is missing $2.3 trillion, a story that evaporated the following day as essential financial records at the Pentagon are destroyed on 9/11.

Between 2003 and 2004, $9 billion went missing from Federal Reserve transfers to Iraq. Apparently, the missing money belongs to Iraq but no one knows who took it. In 2005, whistler-blower Martin Woods exposes massive drug money laundering inside Wachovia Bank. He will be pressured to resign even though the preliminary investigation reveals billions have been transferred into Wachovia by the Mexican mob. The complex court case drags on for years.

In 2006, Felipe Calderon became president of Mexico and vowed to capture or kill the drug lords and their associates, setting off a brutal wave of violence than takes 40,000 lives over the next five years although it will have little impact on drug distribution. In

196

July 2007, the Mexican drug cartels abruptly stop feeding cash into the global banking system (possibly fearing confiscation). Exactly one month later, many notable banks line up at the New York Federal Reserve's discount window for large injections of cash, a sign of impending crisis. J.P. Morgan, Chase and Wachovia all take $500 million. This inadvertently initiates a silent run from major investors that eventually seizes-up the entire financial system. Congress commits around $4 trillion for bailouts, considerably more than the entire cost of WWII adjusted for inflation. The Federal Reserve demands total secrecy but Antonio Maria Costa, head of the United Nations Office on Drugs and Crime, admits that over $300 billion in drug money is used to rescue the system. "This was the only liquid investment capital available," he explains. Costa declines to identify the banks involved and says the drug money is now "part of the official system." (Move along, nothing to see here.)

In 2009, Wachovia finally settles and the bank confesses to laundering $378 billion in drug profits over several years. But they pay only $160 million in fines, which represents less than 2% of their annual profit. During the crisis, the bank is purchased at huge discount by Warren Buffet's Wells Fargo as Wachovia carries $26 billion in toxic subprime loans. Wells Fargo reaps $25 billion in bailout money.

Unfortunately, this is probably just the tip of the iceberg. International banking is a dirty business and has been for a long time. The CIA knows where the money is coming from (third world drug lords) and they know where the drugs are going (organized crime). Apparently, it's not a problem as long as both parties use CIA-connected banks. Over the last few generations, however, the corruption involved in these operations seems to have grown immensely judging by the size of the crimes being committed. One wonders what our real economy might look like without all this thievery to drag it down? Rest assured, banks will

197

continue to pay nominal fines if caught laundering drug money, while most banks will never get caught. Why would they, when no whistle-blower has ever emerged victorious and the taxpayers are always available to pick up the tab?

Scandal in Italy

Although countless masonic lodges throughout the world have undoubtedly participated in political plots, few have been unveiled since Weishaupt was disgraced in Bavaria. The one notable exception is Italy's P2 scandal.

The story starts with the rapid ascension of Licio Gelli to Grand Master of Propaganda Massonica, a lodge recognized by the English Grand Lodge in 1972. Six years later, a journalist and disgruntled member published an article titled "The Great Vatican Lodge," which claimed the Vatican Bank was being manipulated by 121 Freemasons inside the church. The list included cardinals, bishops, and high-ranking prelates. (Since numerous papal bulls had forbidden Catholics to become masons, these allegations were big news in Italy.) While investigating the bank's financial improprieties, police stumbled onto P2's complete membership, which included three cabinet ministers, eight admirals, 43 members of Parliament, 43 generals, heads of all three of Italy's national security agencies, numerous judges, Sicilian men-of-honor, and hundreds of public servants and diplomats. The public officials were forced to resign after the lodge became linked to assassinations, terror attacks, drug-running, and a plot to stage a Fascist takeover of Italy. Their sordid list of activities included the kidnapping and murder of Prime Minister Aldo Moro, and perhaps even the untimely death of Pope John Paul I, who'd supported the investigation, and whose reign lasted a suspicious thirty-three days, the most important number in American masonic numerology.

198

According to a 1993 report on the Sicilian men-of-honor society influence in Italian politics, "The admission of members of Cosa Nostra, even at high levels, in masonry is not an occasional or episodic one, but a strategic choice. The oath of allegiance to Cosa Nostra remains the pivot point around which the men of honor are prominently held. But the masonic associations offer the mafia a formidable instrument to extend their own power, to obtain favors and privileges in every field: both for the conclusion of big business and 'fixing trials,' as many collaborators with justice have revealed."

Pedophile Priests and Mind Control

In 1990, the US version of the P2 scandal threatened to unfold in Omaha, Nebraska, after the collapse of a relatively unknown bank, the Franklin Credit Union. Although this scandal could have brought down the leadership of the Republican Party, news never reached far outside of Nebraska. Most of what is known about the case initially came from *The Franklin Cover-up: Child Abuse, Satanism, and Murder in Nebraska*, by former state senator John W. DeCamp, another book that has sold tens of thousands of copies, despite never being reviewed by any newspaper in America.

After several children in the Omaha area independently revealed to different police agencies that they'd been subject to abuse, torture and illegal drug use, the cases were quietly swept under the rug. But on February 8, 1984, Edward Hobbs, a teller for five years at the Franklin Credit Union wrote a memo to state banking officials detailing massive fraud and improprieties inside the bank, which was controlled by Lawrence E. "Larry" King.

King immediately fired Hobbs, and his allegations would not be investigated for another four years. When the bank was finally raided by federal agents, it was discovered that $40 million was missing. The agents also discovered that King had built a bedroom inside the bank, stocked with child pornography. At the time, King was widely celebrated as the fastest-rising black star of the Republican Party, a man who had been permitted to open the National Republican Convention twice by singing the national anthem. Knight of Malta and CIA head William Casey was Larry King's personal friend and mentor.

By 1990, Gary Caradori, who'd been hired by the banking committee of the state legislature to investigate the case, documented over 30 children who claimed to have been subjected to occult-style brainwashing, sexual abuse and drug addiction. His research revealed that many of the children had been recruited directly out of Boys Town, the most famous Catholic orphanage in America. Warren Buffet, the second wealthiest man in America, has ties to Boys Town, and his wife worked at the Franklin Credit Union.

On June 11, 1990, Caradori was killed in a suspicious plane crash. His briefcase, reportedly containing highly explosive photographs, was never found. However, most of Caradoi's videotaped interviews with the children remained. Here is what Paul Bonacci told Caradori on May 14, one month before Caradori was killed.

"We were picked up in a white limo and taken to a hotel.... Nicholas and I were driven to an area that had big trees—it took about an hour to get there. There was a cage with a boy in it who was not wearing anything.... They told me to fuck the boy and stuff. At first I said, no, and they held a gun to my balls and said do it or else lose them or something like that.... We were told to put our dicks in his mouth and stuff and sit on the boy's penis and stuff and they filmed it. We did this stuff for 30 minutes or an hour when a man came in and kicked us and stuff in the balls and picked us up and threw us. He grabbed the boy and started fucking him and stuff.… The boy was bleeding from his rectum, and the men tossed him and me and stuff and put the boy right next to me and grabbed a gun and blew the boy's head off."

Bonacci was examined by psychiatrists and found to be suffering from multiple personality disorder, a splintering of the mind that occurs when children are subjected to sexual abuse, trauma, or brainwashing.

Enormous forces were mobilized in Omaha to shut down the Franklin investigation. The children were threatened if they did not recant their stories. People involved in the case began mysteriously dying all over Nebraska.

The children had identified many notables (including Omaha's police chief, a prominent judge, and the treasurer of Ak-Sar-Ben, an exclusive masonic-style organization for Omaha's business elite) as being involved in their torture and abuse, but only Larry King would be convicted of child abuse. Strangely, one of the two children who refused to recant spent more time in jail than King, after being indicted on perjury charges by a kangaroo grand jury. According to DeCamp, the mechanism for controlling the jury came from the Union Pacific Railroad, a company built by E. H. Harriman using Freemason Rothschild funds. Harriman's two sons would go on to become members of Skull & Bones. "Executives of the Union Pacific Railroad have been known for two things," remarks DeCamp. "Homosexuality and Freemasonry."

In 1959, 44-year-old Richard Condon published his second novel, *The Manchurian Candidate*. Condon had spent 22 years as a publicist, most notably for Walt Disney. His novel was written after several US soldiers captured in Korea signed statements supporting Communism while in prison camps. Most Americans had never heard of brainwashing until these cases were revealed in the newspapers. Condon detailed some of the science behind brainwashing, but mostly he wrote a savage indictment of America's ruling elite.

The villain of his story was a 50-something Nordic beauty, a member of the Daughters of the American Revolution and the Eastern Star (a masonic society created for the wives of high-ranking Freemasons.) In the book, she mainlines heroin, holds parties for the leaders of both political parties, meets with the Pope, orchestrates multiple assassinations, and employs her 25-year-old brainwashed son as a sex slave. The book created an enormous sensation in Washington. Strangely, no Hollywood studio would touch it.

Director John Frankenheimer heard that Frank Sinatra was a fan of *The Manchurian Candidate* and bought the film rights for very litte. He signed Sinatra to play a lead role, and Sinatra's involvement was the only reason the film got studio funding. When Sinatra called President John Kennedy to tell him the news, JFK had one question: "Who's going to play the mother?"

The film appeared to mixed reviews in 1962. One year later, soon after the assassination of JFK, the book and the film disappeared for 25 years. Why? Because they skirted too close to the truth.

Hoover was the first and only public official to create a masonic lodge inside a federal building. Throughout his life Hoover held ceremonies on Monday nights in his office, and it was widely believed promotions depended on participation in these ceremonies.

After the Franklin scandal erupted, DeCamp was visited many times by former CIA head William Colby, who encouraged the investigation and monitored it closely. Colby had been removed from the CIA for attempting to reform the agency. He had also supervised the CIA's largest assassination program in history in Vietnam, and was the attorney for the Nugan-Hand bank, which had close ties to the heroin syndicate that flooded the US with drugs during the Vietnam War. Colby knew about the CIA's MK/Ultra brainwashing program, undertaken with the assistance of Nazi scientists, and told DeCamp the program had gotten out of control. "Children were only supposed to be used with the permission of their parents," said Colby. Eventually, however, Colby warned DeCamp to get away from the investigation. "This is much bigger than you ever dreamed," he said. "Sometimes things are too big, too powerful, and the best thing we can do is survive. Write everything you know in a book, and then they'll be no reason to kill you.

After DeCamp self-published his book, Colby sent a copy to Attorney General Janet Reno, urging a full investigation, something that never took place. Shortly after making this request, Colby turned up dead.

Today many researchers on the JFK assassination agree that Oswald was a real Manchurian candidate, first subject to mind control in 1955, when he entered the Civil Air Patrol at age fifteen and fell under the command of hypnotist and sexual deviant Ferrie, whose library card would be found in Oswald's wallet eight years later at the time of his arrest in Dallas.

On June 6, 2003, Lawrence Teeter, lawyer for Sirhan Sirhan, the convicted assassin of Robert F. Kennedy, announced that Sirhan had been a victim of hypnosis and mind control and requested a new trial. Sirhan has been incarcerated for 46 years and claims no memory of the assassination, despite having pled guilty in an attempt to avoid a death penalty.

Meanwhile, former Vice President Dick Cheney, a Freemason, is a former director of Union Pacific Railroad. President George W.

Bush is a third-generation Bonesman who flew to the headquarters of the Strategic Air Command on September 11, 2001, where he met Warren Buffet, one of the largest stockholders in ABC and the Washington Post. The Strategic Air Command is located near Omaha, Nebraska, the city with the most documented cases of multiple personality disorder, as well one of the highest percentages of CIA personnel in the country.

I'm a writer, journalist, filmmaker, event producer and counterculture and cannabis activist, and was born and raised in Urbana, Illinois. I started out writing black comedy, but I'm best known as the first reporter to document hip hop and the instigator of the film *Beat Street*. I also founded the Cannabis Cup, organized the first 420 ceremonies outside of Marin County, while launching the hemp movement with Jack Herer and writing some landmark conspiracy articles. Some of my other books you might enjoy:

Why was Lincoln left unguarded when the War Department knew there were serious plots afoot against him? Why was Booth killed when he was locked in a tobacco barn and surrounded by 25 soldiers. Why were two innocents swiftly hanged by a military tribunal and not allowed to even testify in their own defense? You will find the answers in this explosive book.

Does cannabis cure cancer? Cancer is a big subject and easily misunderstood. But there is no doubt cannabis has anti-cancer effects, so why does the US government pretend it has no legitimate medical uses?

In the early 1980s, I became the first reporter to travel to the South Bronx to document the origins of hip hop and my book remains the most authentic portrait of the first generation. It was recently updated with never-before-seen photos and illustrations, and includes everything I published on the subject during the 1980s, including the original script that was turned into the first Hollywood hip hop film, *Beat Street.*

47124912R00116

Made in the USA
San Bernardino, CA
22 March 2017